MANAGING KEY CLIENTS

Managing Key Clients

Kevin Walker
with Paul Denvir and
Cliff Ferguson

PACE
PARTNERSHIP

Managing Key Clients

Published by The PACE Partnership
Copyright The PACE Partnership 2006

For more information, contact The PACE Partnership, PACE House, Churchfield Road, Walton on Thames, Surrey, KT12 2TZ or visit us on the World Wide Web at:

http://www.pacepartnership.com

ISBN 0-9552273-0-5
ISBN 978-0-9552273-0-1

First published 2000 by Continuum
Reprinted 2001 by Continuum
Reprinted 2003, 2004 and 2005 by Thomson Learning
Reprinted 2006 by The PACE Partnership

Contents

Preface: Listening to Clients

Before daring to consider this publication complete and fit for the task for which it was intended, we asked a number of our valued contacts in professional services firms to read the manuscript and to give us feedback on any aspect.

One early piece of feedback we received was from a professional who had read our previous book *Creating New Clients*. Essentially what she said went as follows: 'When a professional read *Creating New Clients* he or she could immediately go out as a sole practitioner and do something that could have impact. The difference with *Managing Key Clients* is that so much of the potential implementation is reliant on other people – usually very senior people – within a firm. I think all of the messages contained in *Managing Key Clients* are spot on – but I wonder if professionals reading the book may come to the conclusion that "there is nothing I can do until the people in charge make some changes around here".'

Instead of just leaving her comments as a constructive criticism, our contact suggested a solution; she said 'Why don't you, at the end of each chapter, finish with some suggestions that an individual professional could implement on his own? In this way every person who reads your book will not only have an understanding of the key principles of effective Key Client management, they will also be doing something about their own way of working.'

We thought this suggestion was worth taking forward. From Chapter 2 onward there is a section at each chapter-end entitled 'First Steps'. These are the types of things that any professional can begin to implement to improve his way of handling Key Clients.

You will notice we refer to the professional in the male gender. For simplicity throughout this book we refer to all professionals as male and all clients as female.

Acknowledgements

As a publication such as this starts to take on its final shape, it is all too easy for the authors to slip into a mindset – believing that the content is 'theirs'. Indeed, we have learned much through our personal experiences gained whilst carrying out consulting and training assignments with professional services firms, and hopefully this learning and experience is reflected in the way we have tackled this subject.

However, we also recognise and appreciate the contribution made through the experiences, ideas and inputs from colleagues. These have helped shape this publication. In particular we would like to thank David McMurdo, Andy Syms, John Monks and Tim Rusling, all of whom are colleagues from within The PACE Partnership, for their contributions and encouragement.

Key Client Management Healthcheck
A diagnostic tool for professional services firms

Before starting to read this book it may be useful to benchmark the practices your firm employs today to look after its most important clients.

The Key Client Management Healthcheck (pages x–xvi) is a diagnostic tool that will quickly give you a picture of those things that your firm does well, those that need some improvement and those that need a lot more work.

Simply look at each statement and compare it to the way things happen within your firm. If the statement exactly describes practice within your organisation, then put a tick in the 'Just like us' column. If the statement does not match practice within your firm at all, your tick will go in the 'Not at all like us' column. The other two columns allow you options if the statement is fairly close to how you do things or if the statement has just a little of your firm encapsulated in it.

The scoring and analysis for the Key Client Management Healthcheck is contained in the Appendix (page 179).

Key:

A = Just like us

B = Somewhat like us

C = Not really like us

D = Not at all like us

	A	B	C	D
1. We have a clearly defined and agreed definition of a Key Client. We have therefore segmented our client base, based on the value of each client to our firm.				
2. The proactive and professional management of our Key Clients is one of the main messages consistently promoted by the people who head our firm.				
3. We have one database for *all* client information.				
4. In our firm, large, complex Key Clients are handled by a dedicated client team.				
5. We have taken the time and effort to capture what our firm really stands for (as opposed to what we would like it to stand for). We have therefore been able to distil and write down the core values of our firm.				
6. The people in our firm who receive high recognition are those people who are excellent at nurturing long-term, fee-generative, profitable relationships with Key Clients. These people are more high profile than technical specialists or new business winners.				
7. We have specific marketing and promotional activities directed toward our Key Clients. These are aimed at enhancing the relationship with these clients and putting us in a better position to win new work.				
8. Our Key Client database is central to the way we manage the relationships with our Key Clients. Anyone inspecting one of our Key Client files would know what we have done with the client in the past, the work we are currently carrying out, the marketing and promotional activities aimed at this client, and what our objectives are for this client in the future.				

	A	B	C	D

9. We educate all of our staff so that they understand the objectives and strategies of the Key Clients for whom they work. Our people also have excellent knowledge of the main market issues faced by our Key Clients for whom they work.

10. Our clients have specifically told us that the marketing and promotional events that we conduct, and which they attend, are markedly better than similar events run by our competitors.

11. All of the people in our firm feel that they own the process of managing our Key Clients. Key Client management initiatives are not just imposed by those who run the firm. We have real buy-in here.

12. We have examined and captured on paper the core values of our firm. Good communication between individuals and a commitment to teamworking are *demonstrable* values for us.

13. With regard to Key Clients our firm is primarily organised in client-facing teams. Functional divisions are secondary.

14. Our professional staff have high selling skills.

15. We have met with our Key Clients and have asked them what they want from a firm such as ours. We have acted on the results of this market information.

16. Our clients understand – and believe – that we have a wide range of deliverable capabilities that go beyond those they choose to utilise today. We have not become 'pigeon holed' by our clients as providers of a narrow range of expertise.

	A	B	C	D
17. Our teams of people who work with major Key Clients have all been trained in the essentials of teamworking and how to work better in a team environment.				
18. For all of our Key Clients we have a plan. This plan has specific, measurable and achievable objectives. These objectives have a time frame, and responsibility is given to individuals to lead in the achievement of these objectives.				
19. Nobody in our organisation ever promises anything we cannot deliver.				
20. Our clients believe in the messages contained in our marketing and promotional activities because they have a very high level of trust in our firm and in all of the people they deal with in our firm.				
21. Our clients have specifically told us that they get value from the marketing activities we conduct.				
22. We analyse who the key people are within our Key Clients and we map out where they are positioned in relation to our firm. On the basis of this analysis we plan how to build our relationships within Key Clients.				
23. For each of our Key Clients we not only have clearly defined objectives, we also have specific action plans that map out who in our firm is going to do what – and by when.				
24. There is a person very highly placed in our firm who has ultimate responsibility for the quality of our client relationships. This person is passionate about this cause and has the 'muscle' to make things happen if it is found that we are not delivering to clients' expectations.				

	A	B	C	D

25. We have a proven and accurate method of forecasting future client work in the pipeline.

26. In order to manage our Key Client relationships in an excellent manner we have identified and written down the key characteristics that our professional staff (involved in working with Key Clients) should possess.

27. All of the people in our firm who have a need, have access to (and contribute to the maintenance of) our client database, wherever they are located.

28. We have a process in place that constantly reviews new types of work we have carried out. This process identifies new expertise we have developed that we could build, repackage and deliver as a new product or service for other clients.

29. We always get in-depth feedback of our clients' perception of the service we are delivering.

30. Those people who are excellent at managing relationships with Key Clients (and who continue to develop ongoing and profitable fee income as a result) receive rewards (including financial rewards) for this activity.

31. Our professional staff believe that the ability to pitch and present powerfully is the core skill in winning 'beauty parades'.

32. With regard to our Key Clients we understand their objectives and know the main strategies they will employ in meeting these objectives. This means that we can link any of our services directly to the impact they will have on our clients or their business.

	A	B	C	D

33. We have made a conscious decision as to what information will be of value to us and what information we should hold about our Key Clients.

34. Internal meetings to discuss Key Clients are seen to be very important in our firm. It is extremely rare for these to be moved or cancelled and all of our people turn up and are prepared.

35. Meetings to discuss Key Clients are well structured and productive affairs. People attending these meetings have received specific training in meeting skills and protocols.

36. It is recognised and accepted at all levels that the proactive and professional management of our Key Client relationships is a business *imperative* – key to the future success of our firm.

37. Our website is more than an electronic brochure. Our website delivers real value to our clients and we have evidence that they return to visit it.

38. We have a procedure for getting feedback on every significant piece of client work we undertake. This feedback occurs both at the end of the work and at agreed and specified milestones.

39. Our base level of service (which every client receives regardless of their value to the firm) is truly excellent.

40. We have objective and measurable ways of knowing the strength of the relationship we have with our Key Clients.

41. There is excellent communication and trust between the different practice areas within our firm.

	A	B	C	D

42. We believe our clients really are worth the effort of nurturing.

43. Our professional staff can correctly articulate the processes involved in successful selling.

44. We always deliver *everything* to our clients on, or before, time.

45. We are comfortable with the concept that different clients will receive different levels of service from our firm.

46. Teams that are dedicated to specific clients work really well in our firm. Good plans are formulated and communication between team members is excellent.

47. For each of our Key Clients where we believe there is a prospect of future work, we have a written action plan that outlines what we need to do to win these specific opportunities.

48. Our professional staff have received relevant training and coaching in how to sell their services and capabilities.

49. The people who work in our Key Client teams can articulate the essential principles that need to exist for a group of people to work together as a team. They can apply these essential principles to the process of using a team of people to work with a Key Client.

50. Our client database contains relevant, comprehensive and updated information on our Key Clients.

51. When our professional staff attempt to cross-sell another of our firm's capabilities, they are always able to give the client the specific benefits of this collaboration *from the client's perspective*.

	A	B	C	D

52. The people who lead our teams that focus on Key Clients are seen to be the individuals most capable of this role – not necessarily the most senior person or the person who has historically 'owned' the client.

53. Our client database integrates with all of our other information systems.

54. We have examined and captured on paper the core values of our firm. Dedication to providing excellent service to clients is a *demonstrable* value of our firm.

55. Our information systems allow us to identify and collate all new business opportunities that are 'in the pipeline' within Key Clients.

56. Our client database has been configured very closely to the specific needs of our firm.

57. When we sit down and formulate our plans for Key Clients we use various tools that illuminate for us what we need to do to develop the relationship (and future fee income) with the particular clients concerned.

58. Our client database allows us to hold both very simple information (on small, 'simple' clients) and, if necessary, very complex and voluminous information on our Key Clients.

59. Marketing and promotional activities are always followed up by our professional staff with a view to generating more face-to-face dialogue with our Key Clients.

60. Our professional staff are really inquisitive. They love to really get inside their clients' organisations and to understand their businesses in depth.

Section 1 **Setting the Scene**

Chapter 1 **Finding the Motivation**

KEY CLIENT MANAGEMENT – A RARELY FOUND PRACTICE

No one disagrees with the notion that excellent client management is important. Good client management means that clients pay their bills, that they continue to give us work and that they include us in their thinking when new opportunities for work arise. Also, the image of being recognised as a client-focused firm is a positive one.

If something is so good for us and for the health of our firms, why is it that most professional firms score poorly in our Key Client Management Healthcheck? Is it because nobody has defined the best ways of managing Key Clients for the professional services sector? Is it because the processes and practices as defined (for instance in this book) are just impossible to implement in a professional services firm? Is it because the support systems and technology needed to support a sound Key Client management process are just not available?

It is none of these.

Addressing the first question, in this book we define in detail all aspects of effective Key Client management, specifically related to professional services firms. The processes and practices have been identified and they are in the public domain.

With regard to the second point, on the viability of implementation, the consistent feedback we received on our first publication *Creating New Clients* could be summarised in the words 'fundamentals . . . common sense . . . practical'. We believe these same words will be used to describe the messages contained in this book. We are not interested in theoretical concepts and interesting (but flaky) psychological approaches. In our practice we involve ourselves in what *works*, in what translates into real implementable ways of working for busy professionals. Our structured but infinitely flexible approach to Key Client planning (Chapter 7) is just one example of this.

The processes of Key Client management are definitely applicable to professional services firms and they are absolutely practical and capable of implementation.

The third question, about systems and technology as an enabler of effective Key Client management, is a particularly interesting one. In some (industrial and commercial) market sectors the management of key customers was carried out extremely well before people had access to computing power. It was done through the application of brain power plus pen and paper. A few years ago it became clear that computer programs – available on PCs and laptops – could replace the pen and paper. A new generation of software products under the banner of Sales Force Automation (SFA) came into being. The software companies who accessed this market early aimed at the most likely targets – organisations that had

- large homogeneous sales forces;
- high costs of selling;
- high belief in the value of their customer-facing people;
- a record of investing in the front line;
- a track record of closely managing both their sales teams and the customers for whom these sales people were responsible.

The professional services sector was a low priority for software firms. However, we would argue that some of these target selection criteria have *particular* relevance to professional firms.

We know of professionals who have examined these IT systems with a view to application within their firms. Almost invariably they have decided not to pursue the issue further: the systems they have seen demonstrated do not fit with the language, culture and ethos of most professionals. Just consider the phrase Sales Force Automation for instance; what professional wants to be part of a sales force, let alone an automated one!?

A common observation is, 'Even if I can see the value in some of the features of this system, we would have a revolt on our hands if we tried to introduce it here.' At this stage the software sales person has tried to reassure the prospective professional service customer that the program can be tailored and customised. However, it is too late: the negative images are too embedded. The professional leaves with the hope that one day someone will have a system that will fit with his business and his people.

That day has arrived. Sales Force Automation systems have developed quickly. As part of this development the badging has also evolved. The new terminology is CRM – Customer (or Client) Relationship Management systems. Perhaps the 'softening' of the name for such systems will help facilitate their introduction more quickly into professional firms. In Chapter 8 we will examine the specifications of an IT system which will support Key Client management in a professional services firm.

These three very common reasons given for the lack of implementation of a Key Client management process do not stand close examination. The practices and processes are defined, they are relevant and practical and the full support of twenty-first-century technology can be brought to aid planning and management.

So what is missing? The answer is simple: it is *will.* In many firms there is not the will and motivation to make Key Client management a reality. There is the desire – sure. People would *like* to look after their clients better, they would *like* to win a greater share of their work, and they would *like* to know that competitors would find it extremely difficult to win work from their clients. But desire and will are not the same things. With desire the imperative is missing.

LEADERSHIP OF THE KEY CLIENT MANAGEMENT PROGRAMME

What is required is leadership. Someone has to decide that managing the client base more effectively is absolutely essential to the future of the firm. He or she has to conclude that the present way of managing things is not sufficient and that changes (possibly major changes) to current custom and behaviour will have to be carried through. This person must then have the ability to communicate this vision to the rest of the organisation and to get buy-in from every level. The energy to then see new processes designed and implemented is required. The ability to empower others who now share the vision and to delegate much of the implementation (without giving away the ultimate responsibility for success or failure) is paramount. The mental toughness to confront those who choose not to buy-in to the new ways of doing things has to be there. The understanding that really effective Key Client management is a never-ending journey – not a destination – also needs to be in place.

These are the characteristics of real leadership; examples of the sorts of behaviours identified by James M. Kouzes and Barry Z. Posner in their bestseller *The Leadership Challenge* (Jossey-Bass, 1995). The person in question must have passion and a belief in this endeavour.

You may conclude that the 'someone' to whom we refer should be highly positioned within a professional firm to successfully carry through the things we have outlined briefly. You would be absolutely right.

The recognition that Key Client management is an essential element of the future of the business must be made by a person who is at the top – or very close to the top – of the firm. If he is only close to the top, then it is vital that this person is extremely highly regarded by senior colleagues and for everyone in the firm to believe that, in whatever he does, he carries the sanction of the managing partner and senior partner.

Too often a marketing manager champions the cause of improved client management. As well intentioned and as well trained as these people may be, when push comes to shove the professional staff go their own way and the non-professional has to work round the idiosyncrasies of professionals who 'know best what works here'. That's how it is in most firms today.

Sometimes the remit for improving Key Client management falls to the person designated 'marketing partner'. In the best situations this person is an individual who has shown some aptitude for developing and managing client relationships. This same ability usually also translates into a person who is extremely busy with client work and day-to-day client relationship issues.

The marketing partner role is something that is meant to fit around chargeable hours (usually the most important objective the individual has to achieve). This person may have the inner motivation to work on improving the firm's Key Client management programme but he does not have the physical time and energy to make any meaningful contribution. It is a part-time role.

The worst-case scenario is the 'partner without portfolio' marketing partner. For some reason no one can quite understand, a wholly inappropriate individual has the title and remit of marketing partner. This person's lack of understanding allied to a lack of motivation for the role means that nothing of value related to improved client management is developed. Any initiative this person may choose to lead carries an image of low credibility. It is rare to find this sort of marketing partner in major firms today, but they have been in place in the not-too-distant past and, in smaller firms, even now.

The person leading the Key Client management programme has to hold a very senior position. The person has to have great credibility within the business. The person has to have the attributes and skills of a leader, beginning with the will to make effective client management a key process in achieving the firm's objectives.

Managing our clients better means managing them differently: we have to change what we do today. We have to change what we may be comfortable with. We may have to change things we have done for years. It is a change process. Our message is the same on this subject as you may have read in countless management texts. To manage change successfully, a business needs many things in place. However, a fundamental element is the existence of a credible champion of change.

WHAT DRIVES THE WILL – AND WHAT GETS IN THE WAY?

The short answer is that it does not matter what drives the will, so long as the will and motivation are strong enough. In our experience, clients often decide to do something about Key Client management because they are intuitively aware that this is not a strong characteristic of their firm. Sometimes some anecdotal evidence of poor client experiences or work unexpectedly lost adds some focus to the desire to 'do something about client management' – or quite commonly to 'train our people in Key Client management'.

Interventions based on such deliberations rarely have much impact. During any training aimed at improving Key Client management, professionals will agree that all the things they are learning about dealing with Key Clients more effectively are good, and that given a perfect world and unlimited time they would see them implemented in their firm.

However, they then go back to the real world and the messages of the real world put client management on tomorrow's 'to do' list.

When our real objectives are all about closely measured chargeable hours, utilisation levels and recovery objectives, the 'soft' goals of demonstrating client-focused behaviour may not appear high on our priority list. In fact giving the client a service that may really delight her and may create an opportunity for 'automatic' follow-up assignments may be counter-productive to achieving today's objectives.

When our position and standing in the firm is (in reality) determined by the level of specialist knowledge we possess or by the prestige of the work we are involved in carrying out, then thrusting effective client management in as another (newly) important value to the firm is not likely to have much impact. In short, Key Client management does not fit well with the real imbedded practices and beliefs of many firms.

Real improvements to the practices and processes of Key Client management come about when the person who is in the position to be the champion of this cause realises that one of the cornerstones of the firm meeting its future objectives is to manage its client resource better.

The objective may be to grow the firm by 20 per cent per annum. The objective may be to build the firm to such a position of strength within the next five years that it becomes an almost impossible (or extremely expensive) acquisition target. The objective may be the opposite of this: it may be to build a market perception that makes the firm appear an attractive acquisition. The objective may be simply to be in business in three years' time.

If the firm is going to truly buy into the concept of Key Client management, then improved Key Client management must not be an objective – it must be a *strategy* which is fundamental to the firm achieving its most important objective(s). A strategy is the broad direction a firm must take in order to meet its business imperatives. It goes almost without saying that a firm that has no clear objectives will have no meaningful strategies. A focus on high quality client management (or any other competitive strategy) will not take root in such a firm.

Assume someone senior within a professional firm had cause to say the following:

> Our competitors are now deliberately targeting our major clients because they see we have weak relationships with them. They are winning them from us at such a rate now that if this continues for another two years the reduction in fee income will mean that we will be loss making and within three years we will be out of business. We must change and substantially improve the way we manage our important client relationships or we will all be seeking new employment.

Now there's a motivation to do things differently! There's a reason to really balance short-term utilisation objectives with time and effort spent in implementing better client management processes.

We do not wish to convey the message that only a severe crisis can be the driver of better client management practices; we do want to convey the message that *something* must be the driver. This something has to be identified by the process champion. This something must be credible and recognisable by people within the firm. This something must be capable of being expressed as a business objective or as a business imperative – an opportunity to be seized or a problem to be resolved. Then we have fertile ground to begin developing the way we deal with our important clients. Then we have the fundamental motivator for the process champion and the underpinning reason for others within the firm to 'sign on'.

CLIENT MANAGEMENT VERSUS NEW BUSINESS DEVELOPMENT

The purpose of the firm in which the authors work is: 'To help our clients meet their key business objectives by aiding them in the generation of profitable fee income.' We can equally help our clients to generate more fee income from existing clients or to help them win new clients. Over the last nine years four out of every five assignments we have been asked to consider by professional firms have been directed at winning new work from new clients. We wrote *Creating New Clients* before we wrote this title because we understand the perceived needs of our market.

As we pointed out in our earlier book, for most firms in most situations creating new clients is the issue we should begin to examine only when

- the current client relationships are so strong we can be 'guaranteed' any recurring work;
- we have positioned ourselves so positively (and widely) within our current clients that they will always include us in any discussions about new work opportunities;
- we have identified all opportunities likely to occur within our current clients in the foreseeable future and we have a plan in place to follow these through;
- we have proactively examined every likely profitable area in which we believe we can sell our capabilities within our existing clients.

If, beyond this, we need to generate even more income, we then have to go out and win new work from new sources.

Given the background that

- Key Client management is not a strength of many professional firms (how did your firm fare in the Healthcheck?);
- very few firms could legitimately claim to have fulfilled the four criteria above;

why is it that new client generation is seen to be so important and existing client management is seen to be so low profile – even when every piece of research work carried out in this area has proven that it is quicker to sell to satisfied existing clients, and it is far cheaper to win work from this source?

True. Indisputable. But winning work from existing clients does not bring accolades and applause, whereas in most firms the generation of new work from new clients is a highly visible endeavour. The people who have proven ability in winning new clients are seen as pioneers and heroes.

The person who gets close to a client and turns a £100,000 piece of work into a regular income of £500,000 a year has had it 'easy'. Such is the common perception. After all, this person was dealing with a 'captive' client. He didn't have to open the door and really sell. He didn't have the same level of difficulty with incumbent advisers. He found it a lot easier to get the key information he needed for the proposal because he was lucky enough to know the right people. In fact, for some reason the client liked his approach so much that she didn't really want to give the contract to the competition.

Huh! Anyone could succeed given those circumstances! This 'new' £500,000 does not have the same value as the same amount of business from a new client.

How do we define value? New work from new clients tends to have a high emotive value. But what about value as defined in a financial sense? It is probable that new work won from an existing client has just as high profitability as new work from a new client. In fact it is likely that the profitability is even higher for two reasons.

First, the selling costs are likely to be much lower. Second, profit is a factor of margin and volume. New clients are less likely to award very large pieces of work to untried advisers. Mostly we will win smaller pieces of work at the outset of a relationship with a new client. As we prove our capability the client will then begin to involve us in larger opportunities. A £500,000 first win may be a figment of our imagination. A £500,000 contract from a very happy, well-managed client may be a realistic win.

Really effective client management is not 'easy' just because some would perceive it as being less difficult than winning new clients. The fact is that many 'hunters' who are good at bringing in new clients are not good at developing the ongoing relationship – even if they would deny this. They find ongoing Key Client management 'difficult'.

RECOGNITION AND REWARDS IN LINE WITH STRATEGY

So what is the answer? The answer is to elevate that which is of critical importance to the firm (at any point in time) to a position of high recognition and high reward.

If it is essential to the future of our firm that we enter a new market sector where we have never had presence previously, then we must put new client developers into the spotlight. The skills of winning new business will be in high demand and those who can apply these skills will be heroes of the firm. If, to build credibility in a new practice area, we must demonstrate leading technical skills, then those who work to develop these skills and deliver our new capability should be our heroes. If our priority is to build our business by working better with the clients that have been built up over years (or even generations) then give recognition to those who do this well. Set targets for it, measure it, identify the best exponents, recognise their achievements, reward them accordingly and ensure that best practice is captured and spread across the firm.

MOTIVATION AND DISCIPLINE AT GROUND LEVEL

If leadership of the Key Client management process is strong and the right reward systems are in place, is this enough to ensure that each individual Key Client service team leader – and everyone on the Key Client service team – has the motivation and discipline to make Key Client management really work within the firm? Our experience tells us not.

In order to achieve success, each person must *want* to carry out the actions that will build strong relationships, especially when some of these actions are not very exciting or visible. Just as in rugby, some players must toil away in the 'engine room' of the scrum while the winger scores the tries and gets all the glory.

Real motivation requires real ownership:

*   *Ownership of the vision* – What does good Key Client management mean and what does success in this area look like?
*   *Ownership of the planning and review process* – If this process is seen to be a 'policing system' people will find ways of fabricating the information and delivering the activities the firm 'wants'. Conversely, if the process helps the Key Client service team leader and his team to be successful (whatever that means) he will use it willingly and all the firm will need do is support and coach him in its application.
*   *Ownership of the values embedded in the Key Client management process* – If professional staff think this initiative undermines the values of technical excellence they hold dear, they will passively resist (or actively sabotage) its implementation. If, however, they really believe it is built on providing the highest possible value to their clients – and can see how it does that – we will receive their active support.

Ownership does not come from being told what to do – especially when, as partners, many Key Client service team leaders are also owners of the firm.

Without motivation, even a passion, for Key Client management, people will always be too busy to do all the things described in this book – too busy, that is, on 'client work', which they thought was the whole point anyway! If, however, they are involved in the design, development and implementation of the Key Client management process, receive effective leadership and appropriate rewards and recognition, and are proficient and confident in the skills to carry out this activity successfully, *then* this initiative can motivate them to feel involved.

However, these people are busy: they have extreme demands on their time from clients and from within the firm. There are many things which will be more urgent (thought not more important) than good Key Client management, whether they are Key Client service team leaders or simply members of a Key Client service team. With the best will in the world, client demands will take precedence over internal meetings to plan and review the actions that will build the strength of a client relationship.

The only way to provide the required discipline for these critical activities is to treat Key Client management as a project. In our training programmes, when confronted with excuses for non-action in this area, the response 'but you wouldn't let that happen in a project' proves impossible to argue. We look at ways of bringing project management disciplines into this process in Chapter 7 of this book. The good news is that it really can be done – with motivation and a project management approach that provides

*   a clear objective;
*   an identified critical path and action plan;
*   clear responsibilities;
*   milestones and a review procedure;
*   strong project management;
*   real teamwork; and (here's the revolutionary part)
*   enough commitment for people to plan their technical work around their Key Client management actions – not the other way around!

SHOULD YOU WORK TO IMPROVE YOUR KEY CLIENT MANAGEMENT?

We can't answer this: only you can. Only you know the vital objectives for your business and so only you will know whether a strategy of improved Key Client management will fit your firm. Only you know how your firm scored on our Healthcheck. If a strategy of improved client management fits with your key business objectives, and if there is room for improvement in your Healthcheck score, then you should go for it.

You will, however, need someone to lead the process.

ARE YOUR CLIENTS REALLY WORTH THE EFFORT?

This appears to be a redundant question: the answer is obvious, isn't it? Of course our clients are worth the effort; but are they? There are firms that focus nearly all their efforts on a small set of high reward and high profit clients, and there are firms at the other end of the spectrum that (usually by default and accident) find themselves with a large set of low reward and low profit clients. For this latter group there is a real question to be answered. Are we starting with a client set that will not only appreciate improved client focus but will also have significant additional profitable work available to win? If the answer is 'No', then the firm has a major job in repositioning. This means winning new clients who have the capacity to provide more profitable forms of work, and being prepared to let go of clients who generate low volume and/or low profit work. Alternatively if we choose to stay in the low profit, low volume end of the market we may then implement a strategy of low cost, efficient delivery with a minimum of time spent in building client relationships and client loyalty.

Key Client development is not a prerequisite for every firm as it is not a strategy that fits every business scenario.

There is another situation where we have seen resistance to the concept of improved client management practices. The counter-argument in this instance revolves not around the value of the clients but the values of the clients. The argument goes something like:

> Our clients may be perceived to be prestigious and they are profitable one way or another but they would never appreciate the efforts we would expend to manage the relationship better. They are a miserable lot. They argue about fees, they invariably change their brief halfway through the work, they blame every setback on us, they try to chisel us at every turn and they pay their bills late. Why should we bother? They should be grateful we do their work and the rest of our competitors should be grateful they don't have to put up with this shower!

There are two ways of dealing with this type of situation.

First, if we genuinely have unpleasant clients that no one in the firm feels comfortable with, then we should change them. Yes, find other clients capable of providing similar financial returns and drop the troublesome ones. Some people find this notion perverse. To those people we would put the question: what would you do if you found out that you were acting for a client who was criminally dishonest? Most reputable firms would seek to distance themselves as quickly as possible. We recognise that dishonesty and unpleasantness are not the same thing. What they both represent, however, is a difference in values. There is no rule that forces us to deal with people whose values we find unacceptable. If we do it purely for the money, then what does that say about our values?

Second, ask why these clients behave in the way they do toward our firm and our people. Is it to do with the way they are – or is it to do with the way *we* are? We have observed on numerous occasions people working within the same practice group who have totally different images of their clients. At one end of the spectrum we have those individuals who feel fortunate and privileged to be dealing day to day with clients who are open, honest and helpful and who appear to try to make work and life easy for the professional. On the other hand we hear from those professionals who somehow seem to have been unlucky to have inherited a group of guarded, deceitful, cantankerous clients who for some obscure reason go out of their way to make life difficult for their advisers.

Our observation is that this is the well-documented Pygmalion Effect (or self-fulfilling prophecy) taking place. People behave as we expect them to behave. The way we treat people determines the way they will respond. If we fundamentally believe that our clients are deliberately difficult, penny-pinching and inconsistent, then they will fulfil this expectation for us. This is not mumbo jumbo 'psycho think'. Robert Rosenthal and Lenore Jacobson, in their work *Pygmalion in the Classroom* (Irvington Publishing, 1992), originally identified the Pygmalion Effect working in schools. The existence and impact of the Effect is now well documented.

In this instance the message is clear. It is the old adage that 'Our clients will get better when we do.'

WILL WE HAVE THE MOTIVATION TO IMPLEMENT ALL OF THE EXCELLENT PRACTICES RECOMMENDED IN THIS BOOK?

Short answer – no. And neither should you, at least in the early days. One sure way to kill off a change in Key Client management practice is to introduce many new and additional ways of working simultaneously. This will ensure the whole process appears so burdensome that the entire organisation unites in a fight against the new regime. We have seen this on numerous occasions.

The most common scenario is that of the new marketing manager who has a background in an industry 'more enlightened' than the professional services firm he has just joined. This person sells his concept of 'bells and whistles' Key Client management to an influential partner who instructs the new manager to 'put it all in writing and we'll instruct our people to do it this way in future'. This is a recipe for disaster.

Given this blank piece of paper, our imaginary marketing manager leaves nothing out of the new Key Client management process: it is perfect in every detail. The partner (who should know better) is sold the benefits of every aspect of the new way of working with clients. It all makes perfect sense – and it never works. There are numerous reasons for the failure. Many have to do with the absence of effective leadership practices, as outlined briefly earlier. However, the single biggest reason is that the busy professional who saw this new monster land on his desk immediately rejected the whole concept as 'too complicated and too time-consuming'. He was probably right.

How do you eat an elephant? Answer – piece by piece. This is how it should be with the introduction of Key Client management processes and practices.

We may choose initially to simply focus on improving the way we sell to existing clients. We may choose to focus on more effective cross-selling. We may decide to implement one tool which will help us think more constructively as to how the client relationship can be built more strongly, or we may aim to put in place the most rudimentary Key Client Plan for our top ten clients. Any one of these initiatives could be a realistic way forward.

Being over-ambitious has serious consequences. Perhaps the most negative effect of a failed attempt is that any subsequent initiatives are immediately greeted with 'We tried that once before but it doesn't fit with our firm, our type of work and our clients.' In fact there may be nothing wrong with the 'new' initiative. The problem may be that the previous attempt lacked realism. Subsequent attempts lack credibility.

In some ways we see the chapters of this book providing a menu. Depending on circumstances, we can all choose what to implement and in which order. We can also choose the pace at which we go forward. The key is to pick the right pace and *continue* to move forward, building on the successes achieved from previously implemented initiatives.

Chapter 2 **Clients, Key Clients and Crown Jewels**

HOW MANY KEY CLIENTS?

A few years ago a client of ours decided that they needed to substantially improve the way they managed *their* clients. A group representing various levels of management and client-facing people formed a committee to agree on best practice and to formalise and standardise best practice across the business.

The client is sophisticated and makes regular and effective use of outside advisers when working in areas where they feel they lack specialist knowledge. In this instance the people within the business clearly felt they had sufficient levels of knowledge; outside input was not considered necessary.

One of the main outputs of this working group was a relationship management plan. The concepts behind the plan were sound. The individual responsible for the relationship had to understand various factors about the client's business and on the basis of this understanding had to formulate objectives. The objectives were based upon ways in which help could be provided to these clients and fee income received in return. We saw the outputs of this work and our client (with whom we have a close working relationship) asked us for our views.

Our views were favourable. We could have argued about detail, but that would have served no purpose. It is far better to have a 90 per cent perfect plan over which a firm has ownership than a 100 per cent plan that has been designed by someone remote – someone who won't be around during the implementation stage. Our real concern came when we asked about the number of client relationships that were to be managed in this detailed way. The answer came back, 'All of them.' At the time this relationship management plan was being devised, each client-facing person was responsible for managing between 45 and 60 relationships. We expressed severe reservations about this course of action, but the plan was implemented across the board.

Despite having had representation on the design committee, the client-facing people disliked the new system. It meant filling in detailed documentation on more than 50 clients. Unfortunately that was how the majority of the client managers saw the new system – as a form of documentation. In time it became a form of documentation that professionals filled in once a year. If a particular enquiry field had an entry and it seemed that the information entered was reasonable, then the professional left it as it was.

With ongoing use it became apparent to those using the system that the most important part of the exercise was that the target numbers entered per client added up to an aggregate figure that senior management were happy with. The bit about really understanding the client's business and spending time thinking about the products and services which would best support the client's achievement of her objectives was lost. The relationship management plan metamorphosed into a sales budgeting exercise; perhaps 'degenerated' would be a more apt description.

Why? After all, this was not the intention of anyone in the business when they first sat down to design the way the organisation should best manage those most valuable assets – its clients. The core purpose of the relationship management plan became lost due to the burden that the plan imposed on its users.

The root of the problem lies in the nature of the implementation. In this instance our client was more concerned with homogeneity and even-handedness than the practicality of implementation. It was considered unacceptable that for some reason one client manager had to carry out the exercise on twenty clients and another on only five. It was also thought to be 'unfair' if some clients had the benefit of having a client manager think deeply about their business whilst other clients were denied this opportunity. It seemed only right that the exercise should be implemented across the board.

The lesson is simple: unless our resources are unlimited, we cannot offer the same level of focus to every client. Any attempt to do so results in a general mediocrity of focus and service. As resources are stretched beyond capacity, compromises are made and the service delivery is also compromised.

CHOOSING KEY CLIENTS

As in the deployment of any business asset we have to make choices and decisions.

In most firms the fee income follows the 80/20 rule: 80 per cent of the income is derived from 20 per cent of the client base. This is a good starting point to begin the debate as to which clients should be treated as Key Clients and which are in the 'Other Clients' category. You don't like the term 'Other Clients'? It sounds demeaning? OK: change the terminology. From now on the category is called 'Valued Clients'. But Valued Clients are still not Key Clients.

The decision as to which clients are designated 'Key' may not be simply decided on the basis of last year's fee income, even if this is a good starting point. Other factors we could take into account are as follows.

The profitability of the work we derive from the client

Some clients may provide large volumes of work, but due to the type of work we mainly carry out for them the work is not particularly profitable. Another reason for lower profitability may be that we are hamstrung by 'competitive' rates negotiated and agreed years ago. We believe we cannot seriously raise our fees to sensible profitability levels without running the risk of losing the client.

On the other hand we may have some clients whose level of fee income is moderate but highly profitable. We could be tempted to include some of these in our Key Client category.

The strategic value of the client

A law firm may see the value in carrying out increasing amounts of work in the Intellectual Property (IP) field. The situation could be that so far it has two clients from whom the firm secures IP work. Whilst the fee income from this work is not significant today, the advisory work obtained from these two clients keeps the professional staff operating in this field sharp and in practice. These clients may be considered strategically critical as the firm seeks to win new IP work from other potential clients in the marketplace. For this reason they may be designated Key Clients.

The reference value of the client

A client of ours has the Bank of England as one of their customers. The value of business from the Bank of England as a percentage of total turnover is insignificant. However, in a competitive marketplace the Bank of England uses our client as their chosen supplier of a particular information service. Yes – they classify the Bank as one of their Key Clients.

The growth potential of the client

Perhaps more important than the value of the fees generated last year is the likely level of fees which can be generated in the future. What is the projected 'lifetime value' of this client? Accountants focused on the manufacturing sector in particular have experienced this over the last few years. The manufacturing sector is shrinking generally, which means that there is less traditional audit and accountancy work to go around. However, there are also a lot of mergers and acquisitions taking place.

If we have a client of moderate size who produces moderate fee income but who is moving down the acquisition trail, the extra effort of treating them as a Key Client may well be worth the effort: we stand to win as they grow. We need to be aware of the other side to this story. Auditors can relate many tales of woe as they have found themselves astride the wrong horse. Their client is acquired and the audit fee and most other income disappear as their contacts and allies are subsumed by the acquirer.

CROWN JEWELS

In the heading of this chapter we refer to Crown Jewels. The meaning of this terminology is probably self-evident. Crown Jewels Clients are a small sub-set of our Key Clients: they are our most precious clients. They are the clients who, if they took their business away tomorrow, would have a significant and long-term effect on our business. Whilst we may in time replace the lost fee income, we may never be able to replace this income from any single substitute client.

Having Crown Jewels Clients may be a two-edged sword. It is certainly a two-edged sword if the relationship is not managed well. A component manufacturer may feel the reassurance of knowing that 60 per cent of his potential output has an almost certain customer – Ford Motor Company. However, this manufacturer must also have a concern about how he is going to reduce his real prices to Ford by 4 per cent per annum. He may also have a nagging doubt about Ford's European manufacturing strategy. Could his business be wiped out overnight by a decision made in the US?

The same principle applies to professional service providers. For instance, over time a technology consultancy may become the *de facto* product development department for a major client. The fees become considered 'guaranteed' and the work is designated 'recurring'. Then one day the client's policy changes. The client wants to run their own product development. They believe they can do it more cheaply. They are concerned over conflicts of interest. They believe they can be more innovative. Maybe someone wants to build an empire and the technology consultancy stands in the way. There could be a plethora of reasons, but the result is the same. The relationship (and the fee income associated with the relationship) is targeted for demolition.

You may quickly react to the above scenario and counter with:

* Someone should have been aware of the discussions happening within the client.
* Someone should have known the client was coming to believe that they were not getting value for money.
* Someone should have known that the client thought the consultancy's ideas were becoming stale.
* Someone should have spotted the empire builder some time before and won him as an ally – not let him develop into an enemy of the relationship.

Absolutely right. And if this fictitious technology consultancy had had a sound Key Client plan and had implemented this plan and generally made every effort to make the people within this organisation feel like Crown Jewels Clients, then perhaps the impending disaster could have been avoided.

LEVELS OF ATTENTION, LEVELS OF SERVICE

We meet resistance to the idea of categorising clients into three sections – Crown Jewels, Key Clients and Valued Clients. The argument for resistance typically goes as follows:

> So what you're saying is that we give excellent service and attention to our Key Clients and absolutely brilliant love and care to our Crown Jewels but the poor old Other/Valued Clients lot – our bread and butter – we just don't bother about. Is that it? Because if it is, I don't buy into this concept at all!

No, that's not it.

First, we would challenge the 'bread and butter' analogy. The 80/20 rule would indicate that our Key Clients are the bread and butter – not the majority who fall into our Valued Clients category.

Second and most important, we did not say anything of the sort. This kind of statement comes from someone jumping ahead and arriving at a 'logical', but incorrect, conclusion.

Let us outline the type of experience that a typical Valued Client may reasonably expect.

The Valued Client (VC) would receive the highest levels of reactive service available.

What does this mean? When the VC phones into our offices she will always be able to speak with someone knowledgeable. She will not spend minutes listening to recorded messages and then press a number that diverts her to an out-of-date voicemail message. On trying to make telephone contact again with the professional's secretary to leave a message she will not be met (constantly) with the secretary's own voicemail message. If she gets through to another person in the department she will not be told, 'I don't know where he is or when he will be back in.' If she is able to speak to the secretary, the secretary will be pleasant and efficient and do all she can to assist the client in her enquiry. The secretary will guarantee that the VC will receive a response by a certain agreed time. The secretary will take it upon herself to deliver upon this guarantee.

When the VC has work that needs to be carried out, the professional responsible will speak in depth with her and understand not only what needs to be done but why and how this work impacts upon the client and her business.

When the professional needs to speak to the VC in person he will never be late for the meeting. He will have spent time before the meeting reading any necessary background material so that he is fully briefed before the discussion. In this way he will not make cross statements which demonstrate quite clearly that he hasn't bothered to prepare properly. By avoiding such *faux pas* the professional will never give the VC the impression that this lack of attention to detail and preparation probably extends to his professional work as well. The professional will never insult the client and waste her time by carrying out background reading in front of her – and then charge her for the time.

Not only will the professional demonstrate a deep understanding of his subject area, he will be able to communicate this in a very human way. He will be able to relate the technical aspects to this VC's situation. He will avoid the use of confusing jargon and he will never give the impression that the VC is an idiot who could not have any comprehension of his specialism. The VC will feel empathy and warmth in her discussions with her professional adviser.

The professional will record and confirm in writing key points and agreements reached in all discussions with his VC. All written correspondence will be in plain English that the client can easily understand.

When the professional is working on the VC's premises he will not spend hours on the telephone handling other client work, then charge the VC for his full time on site.

The professional will not dump part of the technical tasks onto people within his firm who have insufficient knowledge to do their part of the work to the highest standard.

All technical work will be performed correctly and to a high standard first time and on time. All supporting documentation for any work will have a professional appearance and will be meticulously correct in every aspect.

All promises made to the client will be honoured. Any potential variations to the extent or nature of the work will be discussed with the client first, and an agreement as to how to proceed with these changes will be worked out with the client before the professional goes ahead.

All billing will be accurate. The professional will submit clear and accurate records which leave those who carry out the administrative task of raising invoices in no doubt as to how the billing should be presented. The client will never be faced with the task of sorting out the professional's poor administration practices. Billing will never be inflated under the pressure of meeting utilisation levels. The VC will always feel she has received value for the money she is paying.

The VC will be included on any mailing lists that could result in her being sent information of value. She will be updated on any changes within the firm that may have an impact upon her or her business. She will never have the experience of discovering that the professional responsible for her work has been changed and she has not been informed. The VC will receive a 'keeping in contact' telephone call on an agreed timescale basis – even if this is just once a year. The VC will never think she has been forgotten just because she hasn't given us any work for a few months.

The VC will be treated with dignity and courtesy in every contact she has with the firm. The VC will truly feel and believe that she is a Valued Client.

Call them Valued Clients or Other Clients or Ordinary Clients or any other terminology – it doesn't matter too much. What does matter is their experience of our firm. That experience should never fall below the simple standards outlined above.

Valued Clients should receive excellent responsive service. The worry that the introduction of targeted, proactive Key Client management will result in a lowering of service standards for the rest of the client base is ill-founded.

The essential difference between the way we manage Key Clients and Crown Jewels Clients compared to Valued Clients is in the level of proactivity we display. For all the excellent service we may provide for a Valued Client, it is mainly a reactive service. The ensuing chapters in this book are about how we go beyond excellent reactive service and how we deliver a relationship that will have the ultimate effect of generating more profitable work from those clients where the opportunities are greatest.

ASKING THE CLIENT – ANOTHER WAY OF DETERMINING LEVELS OF PROACTIVITY

In 1987 Lloyds Bank segmented its customer base. Its mid-corporate customers (typically businesses turning over between £1 million and £50 million at the time) were handled by a new division called Lloyds Bank Commercial Service (LBCS). A dedicated team of LBCS Relationship Managers managed the customer base. What was new in this arrangement was the basis of the relationship between customer and manager. Banking was taken out of the high street and into the customer's place of business. Common though this may be today, in 1987 this was a radical departure for the banking community.

LBCS Relationship Managers were allocated customers in close geographical proximity (no surprises there). However, they were given just enough customers so that they could probably visit each of them between three and four times a year on average – giving them the opportunity to get to know these customers better and to be able to build a stronger relationship.

Feedback following the introduction of this initiative was very positive and it was not long before the other clearing banks were forced to follow suit. Whilst the other major clearers made progress over the next ten years, independent research showed that the level of satisfaction with the Lloyds service in the mid-corporate market was clearly and consistently ahead of their competitors. Lloyds' only shortcoming was to fail to turn this perceived leadership in relationship management into increased market share. Whilst Lloyds' customers were pleased with the service they received, the customers of competitor banks, in the main, had no knowledge of what they were missing out on!

In 1997 and 1998, with the LBCS relationship management model still clearly the market's quality leader, Lloyds took the bold step of asking their customers what they really wanted from a banking relationship. This research, conducted by an independent agency, was the largest survey of its kind up to that time. Not only were LBCS customers questioned, so also were mid-corporate customers from other banks.

The research findings produced some clear trends. First, it seemed that customers valued a bank that could provide all of the financial facilities of which they potentially had need. Second, there was overwhelming agreement that having one nominated bank manager who was clearly responsible for the relationship with their business was also an imperative.

The third factor which customers agreed on was the need for excellent service – but this is where the divergence of opinion began. Different customers had different views as to what constituted excellent service. The research showed up three clusters of customer types in the mid-corporate market.

The largest cluster was a group of customers who sought fast, responsive, non-intrusive financial solutions from their bankers. They knew what they wanted and they didn't want to be sold products and services because a 'relationship manager' had a target to hit. They also did not value a regular visit from their bank manager. Many of the customers who wanted this type of service ran well-managed businesses and were financially sophisticated. They were not seeking to keep the bank at bay because they feared the bank may discover the worst. When these customers wanted to change their banking facilities they demanded a manager and a back-up system that could provide fast and efficient fulfilment of their requirements.

The second largest cluster valued the relationship and dialogue with the bank manager. However, this group wanted more than a manager who understood banking and finance: they wanted their manager to understand *their type of business* and to have the knowledge and ability to be able to discuss their business in the context of industry norms. The manager had to identify with the critical success factors for their business and to be able to give added value inputs through his or her understanding of the sector in which the customer operated.

The smallest cluster saw their bank in a very different light. This group were very open to input from anyone whom they thought could give new and valuable insights into improving the way that they did business. They saw their bank as a major player in the British economy – an organisation that had resources of which they could only dream. They wanted their bank to bring its accumulated corporate knowledge of business practice, business planning and business systems into their companies and for them to benefit from this supercharged input. They wanted to work with a manager who knew their business almost as well as they did and who would be the conduit to this corporate know-how. They knew that such a service would have a price tag, but if it delivered what they wanted then the value gained would be well worth the financial investment.

LBCS made the 'obvious' decision. They scrapped their top quality, market-leading relationship management programme. They created three new relationship offerings, each one designed to appeal to one of the identified customer clusters.

They went to their customers and asked them what sort of relationship they required for the future. Did they prefer fast, responsive, reactive service? Did they want to deal with a manager who could act as a sounding board and be knowledgeable about their type of business? Did they want to work with a manager who could bring them the corporate wisdom of a financial giant and spend enough time working with them so that he knew their business practically as well as they did?

They focused each of their managers to deal with a set of customers who had all chosen the same type of relationship. They made fundamental changes to the infrastructure of their business and they implemented many new systems – particularly to service the customers who demanded the fast reactive service. They embarked on a vast training programme in order that their managers could deliver to the expectations of the types of customers they were now going to serve.

They could have played safe, and stuck with what they knew, but they bet the company by offering their customers radical service alternatives that had never been considered, never mind seen, before. They had the bravery to offer their customers the kind of relationship that they said they wanted, leaving behind a proven relationship model determined almost solely by the bank.

People often ask how LBCS got such excellent customer feedback for ten years when these customers appeared to be being dealt with through a relationship process which was the ideal model for less than 6 per cent of their customers. The answer is that the customer surveys over the years were focused on what was, on what existed, on what

Lloyds and all the other major players offered. The 1998 survey asked a different set of questions: it asked what customers would *ideally desire* as a relationship with their bank.

The key message emerging from this case study is that the relationship with a client will be made immeasurably stronger if we take the trouble to ask the client what they want from the relationship. What do they really want from us? What do they depict as a successful relationship with advisers of our kind? What kind of dialogue do they wish to have with our firm? How interventionist do they want us to be? How close? We will re-visit this theme in more depth in the next chapter.

We have countless examples when working with client-facing people on our Key Client development training programmes where the team responsible for the client in question takes the 'theory' of Key Client planning and begins the formulation of their objectives, strategies and action plans. They begin to map out how they want the relationship to progress. We can recall very few instances where, when challenged, the team could truly answer the question, 'What will a successful relationship look like through the client's eyes?'

Perhaps before we begin to segment our clients into Valued Clients, Key Clients and Crown Jewels Clients it may be worthwhile raising the subject with those very people who will be the subject of our best-laid plans and most well-intentioned actions.

FIRST STEPS

1. Decide who are the (very small number) of Key Clients and Crown Jewels in your own client list.

2. Examine the way in which you treat your Valued Clients. If there are gaps in the service they receive, plan specific actions to improve this over the next six weeks.

3. Ask your Key Clients (and/or Crown Jewels) what a successful relationship would look like, from their perspective.

Section 2 **Developing the Relationship**

Chapter 3 **Setting and Meeting Client Expectations**

INTRODUCTION

Most professional firms operate in highly competitive environments. They are often competing on fees, especially for large pieces of work. Many complain that clients are buying based more and more on the criterion of price. They claim that clients do not value highly enough the expertise they bring or the hard work they put in.

Some clients – for example many in the public sector – are almost obliged to appoint the lowest bidder. However we would suggest, perhaps harshly, that the reason some clients are so price-sensitive is that, in many cases, the service that they receive does not even meet their minimum reasonable expectations.

MINIMUM STANDARDS

In the last chapter we described the kind of service that we believe a Valued Client should receive. We believe that even this minimum level of service is rare. On a recent occasion when we were in discussion with a professional firm who were a prospective client we made the statement:

> We are never late with anything. Not a letter, a telephone call, a piece of information, a report or any stage of a project. Once we have agreed to a certain timescale we will always stick to it. And we guarantee the quality of the output.

There were quizzical faces all around and a stunned silence. It was as though no firm could make such a statement. It was clearly something that they would not have felt comfortable saying themselves. And yet it is so fundamental. Clearly their clients, and the clients of any other firm who do not deliver on time – every time – cannot trust the promises of that firm. And trust is at the very heart of any professional relationship.

In discussions with other clients who find our views in this area provocative, the next statement they make is often about how difficult it is, how they have to rely on others and how they themselves are always being let down. The thrust of their argument often is: 'That's all very well in theory, but I'm afraid that some delays are a fact of life and happen because of the nature of our business.'

Picture yourself on a platform waiting for a train due to take you to a very important meeting. Two minutes before it is due to arrive it is announced that the train will be delayed by 45 minutes and make you late for your meeting. The announcement includes an apology for 'any inconvenience this delay might cause'. Steaming, you approach an employee of the train company and show your displeasure. His response is one of surprise that you should be complaining and he explains: 'It can't be helped mate. It's the nature of our business.'

Professionals would never use such words, of course, but it is on their actions that they will be judged. Every time anything is late, or sub-standard in any way, *in the client's opinion*, the firm providing the service is giving the same impression as the train company described above. Perhaps clients complain about professional fees for the same reason people complain about the cost of season tickets.

We have highlighted the phrase 'in the client's opinion' because, in this situation, it is the only opinion that matters. However 'fair' or 'unfair' we feel that opinion to be, it is the only one that will influence this client's decision on whether to buy our services again and how much they are prepared to pay for them. If the client *thinks* our service is poor in any respect, it is.

The minimum standard required in delivering to clients must be to at least meet the client's expectation of service, consistently.

EXPECTATION VERSUS 'DELIVERY'

Why are these expectations often not met when the avowed intention of all of the professional firms we know is to give their clients excellent service?

The first thing to note is that most clients are not made unhappy on purpose! In fact many examples of dissatisfaction occur as a result of misguided attempts to keep the client happy. As you are reading this, if you work for a reasonable-sized firm, we would guess that a number of your colleagues are, at this very moment, making promises to clients that they will not be able to keep, however hard they try and however many hours they work to do it. And they are making these promises because they want to make their clients happy – at the *'point of promise'*. They are probably also making promises that are not necessary to make. This is because they do not understand, in enough detail, what the client actually needs and what her expectations really are.

*   Does 'urgent' mean tomorrow or next week?
*   What, exactly, is required for this Board Meeting?
*   Will a draft report do?
*   Which sections are critical?
*   What has the MD been promised?
*   What can be done to help the client to process the information more quickly?
*   When is the last possible time for delivery?

The trouble is that making the client happy at the point of promise but unhappy at the point of delivery leads to dissatisfaction. However, it is tempting to promise what we can't deliver. No matter how much pressure we feel the client is putting us under, the only route to a satisfied client is to make promises that the client finds acceptable (and no more) and then to make that client happy at the point of delivery.

People who *try to be* client-focused tend to overpromise and underdeliver; people who *are* client-focused underpromise and overdeliver. Consider your feelings in the following scenarios.

Scenario One

You are due a new company car: a very nice new car. In fact one that you have always wanted. It is your responsibility to order it from a local dealership, which you do on a Tuesday in late spring. On the telephone the garage promise you that the car will be available for you to pick up on Friday and you put the phone down happy.

You start to think about the weekend. You contemplate a nice drive in the Cotswolds on Saturday if the weather is good. You've not seen your brother-in-law for a long time, partly because he is always boasting about his car, a car that is not half as good as your new one. Perhaps it is time to pop down to see him for Sunday lunch. Maybe you could also leave the car out on Friday night rather than hide it away in the garage.

These thoughts occupy your mind sweetly until late on Thursday evening when someone from the garage phones and, with abject apologies, explains that the car will not be available to collect until Monday morning. Your heart sinks into your boots, especially as you have already made the arrangements for Sunday lunch!

Scenario Two

The same as above, except that the garage promises your car will be ready on the Wednesday of the week after you telephoned and you make all your arrangements for the following weekend. Even better, someone from the garage phones on the Monday evening to say that, if it is convenient for you, you can pick the car up on Tuesday afternoon rather than Wednesday. What fun, the weather looks just right for a spin in the country!

Notice that the actual 'delivery' in Scenario One is better than in Scenario Two – Monday rather than Tuesday – but that the effect is precisely the opposite. Like Mr Micawber who said: 'Annual income twenty pounds, annual expenditure nineteen pounds nineteen and sixpence, result happiness. Annual income twenty pounds, annual expenditure twenty pounds ought and six, result misery.'

We would suggest:

- If expectation exceeds delivery = dissatisfaction.
- If delivery exceeds expectation = satisfaction (or better).

The problem is that even those firms who try their best to ensure that the delivery of their expertise is to the highest standard do not expend the same amount of energy managing the other half of the equation – the client's expectations.

UNDERSTANDING CLIENT EXPECTATIONS

A client's expectations are neither right nor wrong – they just are! If we are to be successful we must meet or exceed them. Blaming the client for having unrealistic expectations is futile and usually denotes a failure on our part in understanding or agreeing her expectations of our performance. It is our responsibility to do what it takes to understand what the client expects.

A client's expectations will be affected by many things, among them:

- Her past experience of the type of work to be carried out.
- Her past experience of us and similar professional firms.
- Our reputation.
- Any input she has had from colleagues who may have been in similar situations before.
- The promises we made when we were selling ourselves!

The last of these factors is the only one on which we have had a direct influence: it is often also the most dangerous.

There are some who think that the professional should do and say 'what it takes' to win the work and then worry about the consequences later. This is a sound strategy if

- the reputation of the firm is not important to the success of the business;
- there is a multitude of highly attractive clients to be won;
- the professional is keen to spend a lot of time and effort in finding more and more new clients who have not heard that the firm 'does not deliver';
- the professional enjoys dealing constantly with disgruntled clients.

In other words, the consequences of overpromising at the selling stage are potentially dire for organisations that want to build a solid future on long-term relationships with the 'best' clients in the market.

We do not directly affect the other factors influencing the client's expectations, but we need to know exactly what they are. The client will judge our performance against them and may well have made promises to other important parties on the basis of them.

Managing client expectations successfully depends on the professional understanding, influencing, setting and agreeing those expectations at every stage of the relationship. These stages include:

- While selling.
- In final negotiations.
- At the start of the work.
- At regular stages in the execution of the work.
- At the end of the project/time period.

We would expect professional people to make a good job of agreeing the 'technical deliverables' of an assignment. However, frustration on both sides is often caused by a failure to agree the 'soft stuff', for example:

- How the two sides are going to work together.
- How they will communicate.
- Who the client should speak to if she gets a little nervous about progress.
- How people can speak off the record.

- How meetings should be run.
- What issues should not be discussed in open forum.
- What the personal agendas are of the people inside and outside the team.
- How information should be presented.

Research into many different types of negotiations suggests that relationships most often break down because of one side's belief that the other side has failed to deliver on the 'spirit' of a deal rather than the letter of the agreement. This is often due to a failure to spend any time coming to an agreement on the 'spirit' when the deal was struck.

It is in the selling and negotiation stage that client dissatisfaction is wired into the project through a desire to win the work and to get on with it quickly.

UNREASONABLE EXPECTATIONS

If the client's expectations are unreasonable, or we are unable to meet them *and* we know what they are at the very start of an assignment, then we have a chance of influencing them. Whether the client will listen will depend on the level of trust we have managed to develop in the relationship. This, as we described in *Creating New Clients*, depends on the client's perception of our

- credibility;
- competence; and
- compatibility.

As we suggested in *Creating New Clients*, this in turn depends on

- Credibility:
  - confidence;
  - initial 'impact';
  - honesty;
  - delivering as promised.
- Competence:
  - knowledge;
  - track record;
  - expertise;
  - searching (non-manipulative) questions.
- Compatibility:
  - demonstrating interest;
  - active listening;
  - adapting behaviour;
  - showing we care;
  - showing vulnerability.

Note the potentially virtuous circle under Credibility. If we have a reputation for 'delivering as promised' then our view on what is achievable is more likely to be taken seriously by the client.

If the expectations are unreasonable and we cannot influence them, the only way to maintain credibility is to walk away from this particular piece of work. This is painful, but much less painful than a client dissatisfied at the point of delivery. Such clients, quite rightly, blame us for the negative consequences of a failure to deliver and may never (really) believe us again.

MEETING CLIENT EXPECTATIONS

Having understood and agreed our client's expectations, the challenge is now to deliver. For this to happen, everyone who is in contact with the client must know exactly what the formula is for delivering to *this* client's satisfaction. Every 'moment of truth', or point of contact, must be managed to ensure that what is said and done at least matches what the client expected.

One disappointment in how a contact is handled may not be disastrous, but every experience will create an impression and it is these impressions which define in the client's mind the quality of service that she is receiving.

Clients cannot be serviced 'by numbers'. Each person who is delivering to the client must *want* to deliver unbeatable service. This motivation cannot be taken for granted.

To some people in professional firms it is the clients who are continually at fault. Clients are considered to be unreasonable and rude. If it wasn't for them, life would be a whole lot easier! Some legal secretaries still appear to believe that their role is to protect their boss from any distractions, even if those distractions come in the form of clients or potential clients. This attitude was less damaging when clients rarely changed their advisers. Nowadays, when clients are determined to get the levels of service that they feel they are paying for, such a feeling of superiority is suicidal. Meeting client expectations is as much about the management and motivation of people as it is about producing a report on time.

How do we know if we are meeting the client's expectations? It might appear obvious that they would complain if we were not. However, all the research suggests this is a poor measurement of client satisfaction. Clearly, if something which affects the outcome of a significant project is going wrong, the client will shout. But what if the client has found it a bit difficult working with one of our people? What if she was kept waiting for information which meant her having to spend more time on the project than she would have liked to? These are little niggles that will influence the decision to appoint us for future work, but each one may not seem important enough for the client to bother to tell us about.

It is essential therefore that at regular stages of the relationship we must find out how we are doing against the client's criteria for the service she expects. We need to ask for feedback. We need to approach this with genuine interest and in such a way that the client feels comfortable in saying what she really thinks. We need to ask *all* of those people who are influenced by our work. We need to ask regularly and not just when we think they will say nice things about us. We need to make it as easy as possible for the client to complain. We need to record their views and check that our understanding of them is accurate. And then we need to do something about them!

A client satisfaction survey and one review every year are very unlikely to achieve the above.

CLIENT REVIEW MEETINGS

In our dealings with professionals over the years we have noticed that the number of hours they are working has increased inexorably. We sometimes feel a little guilty pointing out all of the extra things they need to be doing to build and maintain the client base they want. However, of all the things they could be doing with their time – carrying out work for the client, developing their technical expertise, marketing the firm, selling to new clients, managing their people and so on – we believe that the most important activity (bar none) is the time spent in review meetings with Key Clients.

These meetings should not be seen simply as an opportunity to discuss progress on a project: they can be much more. Here are a dozen things that can be achieved in an effective series of review meetings. The first four of these are concerned with reviewing our service against expectations. The others are discussed in more detail in other sections of this book. We can

- understand what the client likes about what we do and plan to do more of it;
- find out how the project is going from the client's perspective and update the plan for the next stage;
- understand what the client is less than happy about in how we are delivering the service (the 'soft stuff') and agree plans to improve this;
- agree what the client can do to help us to deliver more effectively;
- find out what is going on in the client organisation – current issues, people movements, etc. – so that we are better able to defend our position with the client;
- explore the future as the client sees it so that we are in a position to discuss any expertise we have which might be of value to the client in the achievement of her future plans;
- identify opportunities outside of the expertise we are currently providing and, if appropriate, cross-sell the services of other parts of the firm;
- build a more secure relationship with the people we know on the client's side;
- meet more people on the client's side and bring in more people from our side, thereby increasing the contact surface which is critical to the strength of the relationship between the two organisations;
- make the client aware of the benefits we are bringing to her organisation/ department. She may be fully aware and she may not. Unless the benefits we are delivering are in the front of her mind, we will tend to be starting from scratch in selling our services with every new piece of work we try to win;
- generate referrals into other parts of the organisation and into other organisations;
- show that we care.

With this in mind, it is astonishing that we still meet professionals who are 'too busy' for frequent review meetings and who only carry out those that are demanded by the client.

We would suggest that we double the number of review meetings we have with our Key Clients, and then double it again! And make sure that the client feels she is getting value from every one of them.

EXCEEDING CLIENT EXPECTATIONS

In spite of everything we have said above, client satisfaction is not enough. Most satisfied clients probably feel they could be similarly served by a number of each professional firm's competitors. If the service is perceived to be the same, then the only thing that will differentiate competing firms in the client's mind will be the price. In essence, the firm is providing, and selling, a commodity.

This description does not sit well with many professionals. However, if clients are choosing purely on the basis of price, the situation is precisely as described above – in a commodity market the only differentiator is price.

Choosing a differentiation strategy

There are a number of possible strategies the firm can adopt in this situation:

1. It can become the 'low cost producer' in the market. This does not mean simply selling at the lowest rates. For this to be successful the firm needs to be able to make a reasonable living at those rates. This probably means a combination of finding more efficient ways to deliver the service, reducing headcount, paying lower salaries and getting people to work even harder than they do now.
2. It can constantly invest in developing new expertise which adds greater value to the clients in the market. This will require a focus on innovation and on selling better, leading-edge services for better rates.
3. It can differentiate itself by delivering a totally tailored service that consistently exceeds its clients expectations, thereby generating the optimum level of work from those clients – achieving attractive rates and building a reputation that allows it to secure new clients who will pay well for the service it can provide.

The correct choice of strategy depends on what clients and potential clients value.

If lowest cost is the only criterion then the first option may be the only one to consider.

Where new ideas and approaches are of value and could help our clients' organisations to compete more effectively in *their* marketplaces, the firm may get a good return on the investment necessary for strategy number two.

Strategy three would be appropriate where it would be a good business (and personal) decision for a client to pay more for a firm that regularly exceeded her expectations. This might be the case if this level of service allowed the client to, for example

- reduce her company's input into a solution and hence either reduce costs or redeploy resources where they can produce a better return;

- make and implement plans with greater certainty and confidence;
- gain a competitive edge in her marketplace by being faster to market or reducing costs;
- recommend the use of this firm to colleagues and superiors with total confidence.

The only unacceptable choice is to make no choice at all. If the strategy that suggests itself is unpalatable, then the only option is to find a market that does value the way we want to work.

If option three is your preferred way of working, then it is perhaps comforting to know that in our experience there are many clients out there who would be more than willing to pay a premium for really exceptional service. This service does, however, have to be delivered, and delivered consistently. As we suggested at the beginning of this chapter, too many professionals bemoan their clients' unwillingness to pay the rates they want without being prepared to do what it takes to ensure that the client would never consider appointing a rival, even for a significant reduction in fees.

What then should the firm do to deliver exceptional service? How do we ensure that our clients are, to use a word that is in danger of being overused, 'delighted'? The answers are genuinely easy. In our experience it usually takes no more than fifteen minutes of ideas generation for a group to develop more than enough good initiatives to keep all of their clients delighted for years to come.

Why then are there so few delighted clients around? To check this assertion just note down the names of all of your firm's clients who (you would stake your life on it) would say, if asked, that they were delighted with the service they receive. The reason is, of course, that it is actions that produce delight, not good intentions. Much of this book is concerned with just that – how to make things happen. To conclude this chapter, we will content ourselves with ten key recommendations on how to ensure client expectations are exceeded, and a case study which describes how some of the practices described in this chapter have been implemented with real success.

The recommendations are:

1. Do not rely on an *ad hoc* approach. Create a plan of action focused on delighting this client and then implement it. [See Section 3 of this book for ideas and issues in developing and using such a plan.]
2. Ensure everyone in the firm who has contact with this client understands the plan, is motivated to carry it out and understands how they can contribute to its success.
3. Do not develop a generic 'client delight plan'. Build an accurate understanding of *this* client's issues, needs, expectations, etc., and develop a plan tailored to adding value to this specific client and to making sure she is, and continues to be, delighted.
4. Allocate a specific budget in time and money to delighting this client. This should form part of the firm's marketing budget and should compete with other uses of this budget. We should not try to carry out this activity in our 'spare time'.
5. Plan to delight the *people*, not just the client organisation. Build this plan on a deep understanding of the personal agendas and likes and dislikes of the key people in the organisation. Add value to each of them in the way that will have the greatest effect.

6. Underpromise and overdeliver on all of the 'little things'. It is these that create an impression within a relationship.
7. Build a genuine interest in the client's (and each person's) business. Keep up to date with what is going on in the company and in their market. In this way ideas to add value will be easy to find.
8. Train everyone who is involved in review meetings and in other contacts with the client so that they have the skills and confidence to exceed the client's expectations every time.
9. Spend ten minutes, and only ten minutes, every week thinking up ideas on how to surprise, and delight, this client with some action beyond her expectations.
10. If any of the above would be additional to the effort we already put in, and if our time is already fully occupied, we should not devise a plan based on these ideas before we have decided, in detail, what we are *not* going to do. What actions are we going to give up that will leave space for these actions? If we do not make space we will end up with a 'wish list' and a client receiving the same old service they can get from a number of our competitors.

If achieving success in setting and exceeding client expectations sounds a little like hard work, it probably is. Success in ensuring that clients keep coming back is created through 5 per cent inspiration and 95 per cent perspiration. The following case study shows that it can be done and the rewards that can be gained by doing it well.

● ●

The ICI Colours and Fine Chemicals Story

Perhaps our favourite illustration of Key Client focus and of delivering to the client's expectations is a story that goes back to 1989. The organisation was ICI Colours and Fine Chemicals. In the 1980s this part of the ICI empire was a laggard. On practically any measurement it performed badly compared to its main Swiss and German rivals. It was a typical production-focused British company – and it lost money.

A new management team led by Tony Rogers (Chairman) and Mike Parker (General Manager) took over the business in 1987 and set about transforming the practices and fortunes of this international business. They instigated a number of initiatives aimed at changing the whole mindset and way of working within Colours and Fine Chemicals. Some of these initiatives were internally focused and a number were aimed at ICI's customers.

The initiative of particular relevance to meeting clients' expectations was the Customer Charter. ICI knew it had a problem with customer satisfaction: they had known this for some time. At one meeting where the management team were wrestling with this issue, Mike Parker uttered the words: 'Customer service is like sex. There are a hundred people talking about it but only two doing it.' ICI were committed to stop the talking and start delivering. Their main objective was to achieve and sustain a highly visible zero defect performance.

Market research had provided ICI with the feedback that customers valued seven key deliverables. These were:

1.   Product quality.
2.   Delivery (on time and complete).
3   Quality of communication.
4.   Quality of documentation.
5.   Quality of complaint handling.
6.   Quality of technical support.
7.   Quality of visits (principally by the account managers).

These later became known as the Seven Pillars of Quality.

From this research and the commitment to do something about customer satisfaction, ICI created its Customer Charter. The Charter had three parts:

1.   *The Service Package Agreement*
     This defined the performance standards agreed with the customer.

2.   *The Audit Report*
     This reported the customer's view of ICI's precise performance against the defined standards.

3.   *The Corrective Action Plan*
     This provided a fast, responsive programme to eliminate at source any defects in ICI service performance.

This part of ICI had 3,000 customers, worldwide, at the time. They focused implementation of the Customer Charter on 500 Key Customers, 70 of whom were defined as Gold Key (the equivalent of Crown Jewels).

Key Customers were introduced to the concept of the Customer Charter by their account manager and were asked if they wished to participate in the programme. There was universal acceptance by customers. Customers were then asked to rank the Seven Pillars of Quality and award points (out of 200) to each of the elements. Part of ICI's research had shown that different customers valued each of the Seven Pillars to different levels. A manufacturer that had its own in-house technical support was not likely to value this 'Pillar' highly. However, a smaller organisation without this facility would be heavily reliant on ICI's technical capability.

A discussion always ensued as to exactly what the customer was seeking with regard to each of the Seven Pillars. The outcome of this discussion and the points awarded formed the basis of the Service Package Agreement. In the words of Mike Parker, this made ICI's Customer Charter 'much more believable – because it came from the customer'.

Whilst ICI did its best to meet a customer's expectations on a daily basis, every six months the customer's people were asked to compile the Audit Report. This formed the basis of a discussion between the customer and ICI. This was rarely a meeting just between the buyer and the account manager. The people who had contributed to the Audit Report were present from the customer's side, and ICI fielded their most appropriate team for the occasion. The result was a round-table dialogue between customer and supplier – both working together to try to find ways of improving the quality of the relationship, both working to define more clearly the customer's expectations, and both working to meet those expectations.

The physical output from these meetings was the Corrective Action Plan. Interestingly, the Action Plan nearly always involved actions from both sides. A round-table problem-solving dialogue could (for instance) diagnose that one reason for delivery problems was poorly defined or late orders submitted by the customer's buying department.

However, the outcome delivered much more than a Corrective Action Plan. Key Customers were extremely impressed by a company committed to trying to be the best. The communication and links between ICI and its most important customers were made immeasurably stronger. (For more on this and how to measure the strength of relationships with customers see the Relationship Protection Index in Chapter 7.)

Most importantly, it had a huge impact on business between Colours and Fine Chemicals and its customers. Looking back ten years after he introduced ICI's Customer Charter, Mike Parker describes the programme as 'an overwhelming success measured from a sales perspective'.

Picking up on the Seven Pillars concept, a number of ICI's customers took the principle to **their** customers and built competitive advantage for themselves using this same way of defining and delivering to customer expectations.

• •

We are always pleased to have the opportunity to tell the ICI story. In the early days of the Customer Charter roll-out, consultants from our firm knew all of the details but were not allowed to reveal how this division of ICI was making big inroads into its competitors' market shares, such was the magnitude of impact of this initiative. The break-up of ICI, the formation of Zeneca and the passing of a decade now mean that this illustration is no longer market-sensitive. In fact it is a story that Mike Parker and his team of the time are proud to tell. Along with a number of other customer-focused initiatives, this management team turned the business around and the organisation became highly profitable.

Perhaps it is easy for a professional firm to dismiss this story as 'irrelevant': after all, it is many years old and it relates to a manufacturing business. We would suggest that professionals inclined to this way of thinking should pause and consider the following question. If a selection of our clients were asked today what are the key areas of service delivery in which they expect us to excel, how different would the top seven answers be when compared to ICI's Seven Pillars?

We believe the ICI story is very relevant and very contemporary. We hope one day to have such a powerful illustration concerning a professional services provider.

FIRST STEPS

1. Make sure that there is absolute agreement with your Key Clients on the expectations they have of the work you are currently carrying out for them.

2. Ensure that these expectations can and will be met. Communicate these expectations to all of the people in the client service team.

3. Agree the 'soft stuff' deliverables in the relationships with your Key Clients.

4. Organise a wide-ranging review meeting with each of your Key Clients. Plan to ensure that these clients will get real value from these meetings.

Chapter 4 **Marketing to Clients**

A FEW DEFINITIONS AND STARTING POINTS

Before we begin to examine effective marketing techniques aimed at clients, it is important that we define some basic parameters – a few definitions and assumptions which will underpin the ideas which follow.

Marketing

Marketing experts would argue that a lot of people within professional services firms either misunderstand or misuse the word 'marketing'. Within professional services the word is usually synonymous with the term 'promotional activities'. Ask most professionals what their marketing people are charged with doing and they will tell you that they organise seminars, set up entertainment activities, arrange mailshots, buy in mailing lists, try to build a database for future marketing activities and co-ordinate brochure production and printing. In some firms the marketing people are seen as a valuable asset to be used in proposal support.

In contrast, the marketing professional within a sophisticated commercial company would put forward the view that marketing was the prime function concerned with the strategic positioning of the business in its marketplace. She would argue that marketing was about using the tools of market research, new product development, distribution, channel management, direct response, promotion and advertising, and pricing strategies. She would also say that the sales organisation was an extended arm of the marketing function.

She would be correct. Marketing in the twenty-first century is about all these things.

For the comfort of the majority who will read this book we will stick to the typical professional services view of marketing. If the experts want to accuse us of focusing purely on promotional tactics then they have every right to do so.

However, from this point on, marketing is about the activities of advertising, sponsorship, running business clubs, seminars, business breakfasts, themed lunches, sponsorship, entertainment and so on.

Clients

What is a client? The question is not so stupid as it first appears. For the purpose of our examination of marketing activities we will define a client as:

A person (we accept that there may be more than one person) for whom we have carried out paid work within the last twelve months. The work we carried out for the client met, or more than met, her expectations.

You may see now why we want to define a client. The effect of any marketing activity will probably be influenced by the length of time since the client (and her organisation) had the opportunity to experience the quality of our work and expertise. There is nothing magical about the twelve-months cut-off: we have chosen this arbitrarily. However, every firm should have a time period after which it is decided that a 'client' has become dormant.

Our definition specifies that a client is someone (or a number of people) for whom we have direct experience of carrying out work. So what about the manager within the same organisation (who could also provide us with work, but whom we haven't met) whose office is on the next floor? Answer – he's not included. Under the heading 'New contacts, existing clients' later in this chapter, you will see why.

We have also included the caveat that the last (or current) work we carried out was of a good quality.

We do not believe that these constraints on the definition of a client are unreasonable. Putting them in place allows us to focus on mainstream situations rather than trying to suggest appropriate marketing approaches aimed at 'clients' who haven't dealt with us for five years because last time we got the work totally wrong, insulted the chairman personally and ended up in litigation.

The aim of marketing

The aim of marketing to clients is to expose them to the wider capabilities of the firm so that they will consider us for new and additional fee-earning work when the opportunity arises within their businesses.

We have not made reference to convincing the client to consider us for more of the same work we have done in the past. Under the heading of 'The negative effects of a positive image' later in this chapter we will expand on why this is so.

The clients' view of marketing

In the chapter 'Attracting new clients' in his *Managing the Professional Service Firm* (Free Press, 1995), David Maister writes that the professional services clients for whom he works worldwide have reached a very definite conclusion as to what their clients perceive as effective marketing.

> Clients measure the effectiveness of any professional services marketing by the level of value they obtain from it. A successful marketing tool will *give* something to the client.

Not a radical conclusion really. The client is saying that if you want me to believe that you are a professional firm that can add value to other parts of my business – should I commission you to do additional work for me – then demonstrate this. Show me. Prove it to me.

The basis of what follows is now set.

1. Marketing is synonymous with promotional activities.
2. A client means someone who has used our services recently and is reasonably positive.
3. The aim of marketing is to put us in the position to win additional new work.
4. Clients are likely to respond best to marketing activities that provide value for them.

WHY MARKETING TO CLIENTS SHOULD BE EASIER – BUT OFTEN ISN'T

The prospective client scenario – needs, wants and trust

In *Creating New Clients* we showed that the theory of needs-based selling leaves too many buying decisions unsatisfactorily explained. In the chapter entitled 'Selling – the Art of Persuasion' we examined the full set of reasons why people are persuaded to take one course of action rather than another. It became clear why people chose to work with one firm of chartered surveyors when technically there were at least half a dozen other firms who appeared equally capable of doing as good a job.

The reasons for a decision to use one firm and not another can be complex. However, there are three essential criteria that a firm must be able to fulfil to win work from a new client.

First, the firm and its people must possess the technical abilities to perform the work to a high standard that will be acceptable to the client, and they must also be able to communicate this to the client. The firm has to be able to prove that it can meet the client's logical, rational, measurable needs.

Second, the people representing the firm to the prospective client have to meet the emotional wants of the people who will make or influence the decisions as to which advisers are chosen. For example, some clients want solutions that are safe whilst others want to be seen as 'leading edge'. Some want solutions that do not involve them personally in extra work whilst some want solutions where they will be involved and informed every step of the way. Some want solutions that will reflect well on their chosen image – whatever that may be.

Few of these decision-making criteria ever appear in the Invitation to Tender and such criteria expressed in writing could be extremely embarrassing for the individuals involved. But just because these factors are not committed to paper does not make them any less real. Anyone who has worked closely with clients over a period of time will have observed that people's personal wants, prejudices and ambitions can have a huge influence on the decisions they make. This applies just as much to business decisions as to personal decisions. The only difference is that in business, people are more careful to justify and rationalise those decisions that are heavily influenced by personal preferences.

So we not only have to fulfil the logical needs, we must also meet the emotional wants.

The third criterion that must be satisfied is trust. A prospective client may believe we can meet the technical needs related to a piece of work. We may even have been astute enough to pitch our response in such a way that it rang true with some of the less tangible wants of the people involved in the decision, but . . . do they trust us?

We have unbundled the factors that contribute to building a relationship of trust. We must build an image of Credibility and Competence and we have to be able to demonstrate real Compatibility with our prospective client. In *Creating New Clients* we delved further and explored the specific behaviours that influence, in the prospective client's mind, the perception of Credibility, Competence and Compatability. We also made the point that it often takes time and many interactions with a potential client before she is comfortable that we have proven our trust credentials.

So, if over time we can prove our trustworthiness and then have the opportunity to bid for a piece of work where we can put forward a technically excellent solution which also hits the right emotional notes with the right people, we are in the frame for winning new work.

New contacts, existing clients

We made reference earlier to trying to win work from new contacts within existing clients. In most instances we would suggest managing these approaches in the same way as we approach totally new prospective clients. Trust is built with people – not companies. Any professional who has been on the winning new business trail must have met the situation where he has had a 'lead' into a new part of an existing client – and been met with hostility and scepticism from the outset.

The simple fact of having previous association with a poorly regarded part of the client's organisation is reason enough to raise question marks in the new contact's mind ('If you fit in there you're not very likely to fit in here!').

We are not suggesting this is the norm. However, unless our provider of the introduction is considered to have very high credibility and influence by the new contacts to whom we have been referred, we should be happy if our initial reception is one of open-mindedness. We should seek to build trust and understanding with our new contacts at a pace they are comfortable with. The strategy is much more akin to creating new clients than managing Key Clients.

The client scenario

We have met some professionals who have disputed the premise that it is easier and quicker to sell more services to an existing client than to a new client. These people were not being perverse and argumentative for the sake of it, they were expressing an opinion based on experiences.

It *should* be easier to sell more to an existing client. (Remember in our definition we stated that the client's expectations of our previous work must at least have been met.) The underpinning reason why it should be easier is that in conducting our earlier work with the client, we should have built hugely our position of trust. Conversely the problem with selling to prospective clients is that we are trying to build trust without the client having the opportunity to totally feel how it is to work with us. When we have carried out work for the client, this barrier is largely removed.

With an existing client we should have demonstrated high competence by the way we approached and carried out our work and through the knowledge and expertise we brought to its execution.

We should have built Credibility through being seen to always be scrupulously honest and transparent in our actions and through always delivering what we promised, on time.

We should have demonstrated Compatibility by proving how adaptable we are when dealing with different individuals, by demonstrating real interest in the client's business (beyond the specific work we carried out) and by showing we cared in a hundred and one little ways.

Trust we should have.

The negative effects of a positive image

With the biggest hurdle to winning work reduced to almost nothing, why is it that some professionals *still* claim it is difficult to sell to existing clients? Surely if we have done such an excellent piece of work and the client now likes us and trusts us, they are likely to use us to do the same again?

True. We may even become an automatic choice in future. If we continue to perform well then why would they ever want to change advisers?

But what about winning *different* work from the same client? This is where the situation changes. When we dig deeper with the professionals who contest the notion that it is easier to sell to existing clients, they always relate stories of trying to sell new or different services or capabilities to those that the client has used from their firm previously. They have no problem with the premise that it is easy to sell more of a proven capability to an existing client. This is not their problem.

An engineering consultancy firm with whom we have worked for a number of years had consistently won project management work from a major oil company. The relationship between the two businesses was very good and the consultancy had a virtually continuous fee income from their client.

A change in management led to the implementation of a plan to widen the type of work won from this oil giant. The new management could see a host of potential opportunities which competitors were awarded and which their firm never had the opportunity to bid for.

Our client put their name forward to be considered for environmental impact assessments, strategy reviews and a number of consultancy projects. On only one occasion did they reach the shortlist. Standing back as a neutral with all the information to hand, one could conclude that life was being unfair to our client. They definitely had the skills and capabilities within their firm to carry out this new work they were proposing for. They had a successful track record in all of these areas with other clients. The problem lay in the client's head.

Al Ries and Jack Trout have written a number of best-selling and highly readable books on the subject of marketing. *Marketing Warfare* and *Positioning* (both McGraw-Hill, 1985) are two of their better-known titles. The underpinning message in all of their work is that what we are as an organisation is what we are in the client's mind: nothing more, nothing less. No other perspective matters. It is not an issue of fact, it is not an issue of statistics: it is an issue purely of belief and perspective.

Ries and Trout's books are illustrated with dozens of examples that demonstrate this point.

The fact that our client was such an excellent provider of project management expertise did not work in their favour when they wanted to pitch for a management consultancy project: it worked against them; it pigeon-holed them. What did project managers know about management consultancy anyway? What made the stereotyping even more pronounced was the fact that they had a track record of over ten years as trusted project managers with their oil company client.

We see this picture constantly. In one client a law firm is pigeon-holed as a provider of litigation advice and the client would never think of them as advisers on licensing. Within another client organisation that makes extensive use of the firm's licensing expertise, they would never make the connection that the firm was extremely capable in handling corporate work.

The frequency and quality of cross-selling carried out by professionals within the firm will have an effect on this lack of understanding from the client. However, simply improving the cross-selling (which we will examine in Chapter 6) by itself will not totally address the issue. There is an image problem.

We believe that the prime function of the marketing effort aimed at existing clients is to demonstrate the images that the firm wishes to build in the client's mind. The pluralisation of the word 'image' is deliberate and critical; so is the choice of the word 'demonstrate'.

To return to our earlier aim of marketing:

> The aim of marketing to clients is to expose them to the wider capabilities of the firm so that they will consider us for new and additional fee-earning work when the opportunity arises within their businesses.

THE 'NEARNESS TO CLIENT' PYRAMID

In *Creating New Clients* we introduced this model for professional service firms' marketing. Broadly, we break down marketing activities into three main categories. These are:

1. *Corporate Marketing activities*. These activities build the image of the firm and create a general awareness of what we do.
2. *Capability Marketing activities*. These activities illustrate the specific capabilities of the firm.

3. *Contact Marketing activities.* These activities demonstrate the added value that the firm can provide and show how it differentiates itself from the competition. These activities nearly always involve interaction between the client and people from our firm.

Figure 4.1:   The 'Nearness to Client' Pyramid

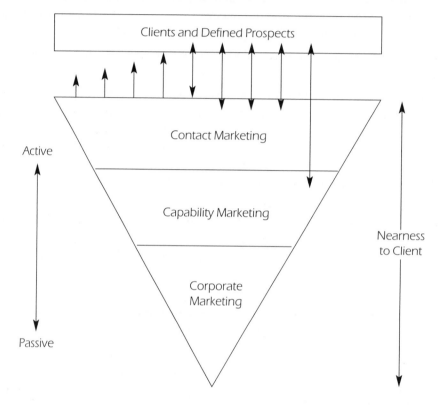

As the model in Figure 4.1 graphically illustrates, Contact Marketing activities involve direct client interface whilst Corporate Marketing activities at the other end of the pyramid are often impersonal and happen at a distance from the client.

Contact Marketing activities are active, whilst Corporate Marketing activities are largely passive.

Corporate Marketing to clients

Corporate Marketing activities typically include such things as corporate advertising, sponsorship, public relations and the production of corporate brochures. Public relations encompasses TV, radio and press interviews, press releases, articles written about the firm and advertorials. A more recent Corporate Marketing exercise is called product placement. This consists of having the firm's name prominently displayed at some points in a commercial movie. This trend began with fast-moving consumer goods companies (e.g. Coca-Cola) and moved on to manufacturers of consumer durables (e.g. BMW). Professional service firms have now added this form of corporate promotion to their marketing basket.

It is easy to dismiss Corporate Marketing as a waste of money – and we have heard plenty of front-line professionals describe it thus. Most Corporate Marketing activities certainly do cost large sums. The simple argument used by professionals who see little value in Corporate Marketing is summed up in the words of one accountant we spoke with recently. He said, 'Why do we bother spending all this money trying to create broad awareness with our clients. They know us already!'

There are two answers to this. First, the whole world was not his firm's client. Despite working for a large firm there were far more non-clients than clients within the market sector in which this professional operated. Therefore Corporate Marketing has value in keeping the firm's name in front of non-clients.

Second, Corporate Marketing has some value with existing clients. Hearing your firm of advisers interviewed on radio is reassuring. Seeing your advisers sponsor a valued business award is warming. Reading an article that quotes your personal adviser is positive affirmation that you have chosen a reputable and well-regarded firm of advisers.

Imagine the opposite situation. Your advisory firm is never asked to give their opinions on radio or television, they are never involved in sponsoring valued awards and their name never appears in the press. However, their main competitors achieve all of these things. Would this affect how you feel about your firm of advisers and their position in the marketplace?

Some to whom we have put this question have answered with a definite, 'No, it wouldn't, so long as they were doing an excellent job for me.' Others have seen the point we are trying to make.

Where a firm can go wrong is through concentrating too much of its marketing efforts into Corporate Marketing activities – in the belief that spending a lot of money equates to achieving marketing effectiveness.

Sophisticated firms understand that Corporate Marketing activities are only a part of the mix. However, not long ago we visited a firm of architects and learned that the previous year's marketing effort consisted of producing a magnificent brochure (sorry, book!) which cost over £20 per copy!

Capability and Contact Marketing to clients

It is perhaps not surprising that if we are attempting to prove our capability to clients in areas of expertise in which they have never previously associated us, we are going to have to use Capability Marketing. Capability Marketing activities include speaking at conferences, writing 'technical' articles in the trade-orientated press, publishing newsletters and carrying out surveys and research into topical issues in which we have expertise and our clients have interest. We are demonstrating our capability to clients – even though we are not in face-to-face dialogue with them.

Contact Marketing activities are those which give us the opportunity to interact with the client and to demonstrate that we can add value. Discussion groups, business breakfasts and themed lunches are examples of Contact Marketing activities. The essence of these activities is that we spend time with a small number of clients and have the opportunity of discussing a particular subject and how that subject impacts upon their business. We specifically demonstrate how we can add value to the client and her business.

What about seminars? Where do they fit? Whilst our 'Nearness to the client' pyramid has a neat line between Capability and Contact Marketing, the real world is not that simple. A seminar could fall either side of the line. Let us illustrate.

Seminars – Capability or Contact Marketing?

Two competing law firms (we will call them Firm A and Firm B) decide to run a seminar for clients who are likely to be affected by an impending piece of employment legislation. Both realise that if they can get an audience of decision-makers together and outline the ramifications and potential impact of the new law, they stand to win a lot of subsequent work.

Both firms also realise there is an opportunity for raising awareness through a short seminar and demonstrating capability in this area without 'giving the shop away' and providing free advice. Both conclude this is a marketing exercise. There will be no fee for the seminar. Participants will leave with enhanced knowledge of the issues and the steps they need to take, but they will not be able to take those steps without engaging the services of a lawyer.

The Firm A scenario

In Firm A a mailshot is prepared and a mailing list is bought from a mailing house. The list is substantial as the firm is concerned about attracting the right numbers to make the event worthwhile. In fact the mailing list is so substantial it would be impossible to check it. Regretfully the Marketing Assistant has to abandon any attempt to personalise the salutation at the top of the invitation. The letter goes out addressed 'Dear Business Colleague' – even to long-standing clients.

Over the next three weeks replies arrive reserving places on the seminar. A total of 85 are received. Firm A is very pleased with the response. The seminar is designed and the speakers rehearse their parts. It seems the delivery will be very professional. A week before the seminar is due to run, the Marketing Assistant chases the Managing Partner for the names of the people who will be available to attend the seminar to talk with the clients and prospects. A couple of days later an e-mail is sent to all professional staff asking who is available on the day in question. The Marketing Assistant is sent the list of people who can help on the day.

He is not filled with joy. The people are mainly junior and he knows that a number are individuals who find it difficult to find work – partially because they are not good at marketing and selling themselves. He has a total of eight to support. Only one associate specialises in employment law; the others come from an assortment of disciplines.

The day arrives. The Marketing Assistant turns up early at the hotel to find the venue totally organised. The conference room is all set up, all of the audio-visual equipment is of the right specification and the reception area is prepared exactly as ordered. The presenters turn up early. They are satisfied with the room and equipment and begin their final preparations.

A couple of host professionals arrive. The participants begin to arrive in numbers. Three more professionals arrive. The professionals mill with the participants asking them how they found the journey and talking about how nice it will be when the weather gets warmer and oh! on the subject of warmer weather, where are you going for your holidays? After a short while most of the professionals find someone to talk with who is amenable and not at all threatening. Before you know it, it is time for the seminar to begin.

The 40 participants enter the conference room which is set out for 85. As they make themselves comfortable many are thinking, 'Why didn't all these others turn up? Do they know something I don't? This doesn't look good – it seems that over half the chairs are empty!'

Most of the supporting professionals don't attend the seminar. It is not a subject in which they have an interest after all. The seminar finishes on time, just before the scheduled light buffet lunch. The speakers have presented their subject professionally. They were clearly expert in their field. All participants agree that the presentation and question-and-answer session were somewhere between useful and extremely useful.

Four professionals plus the speakers attend lunch. Some of the professional staff who attended the morning opening find themselves 'unable to stay to the end' and others 'didn't realise that it was a whole morning event'. On the plus side, a couple of others arrived after the seminar got under way. They 'didn't expect the traffic to be so bad' so they make up the numbers a little. Two who were meant to attend just never show up: no one is sure why.

Lunch is pleasant. The professionals are true gentlefolk. They allow their guests to go to the buffet first and then they make their way to the food. By the time the professionals have filled their plates the participants have formed tightly bunched groups and are engaged in animated conversation. This is not too much of a disaster as it lets the professionals form their own discussion group. Thirty minutes later the participants begin to leave. Most turn to the presenters to shake their hands and thank them for a very interesting morning.

When the participants have all left, the professional staff make their way back to the office and record a few hours of marketing activity on their time sheets.

The Firm B scenario

In Firm B a 'similar' set of activities occurs. The firm's single client database is interrogated for a list of senior people responsible for employment issues within existing clients. For those clients where this information is not held, a brief telephone call is made to find the name of the person concerned. The prospect database is also interrogated in the same way.

At the same time the professional staff are briefed on the purpose and objectives of the forthcoming seminar. Their support is sought early and their role in aiding the success of the seminar is agreed. The mailing, inviting people to the seminar, is despatched to a targeted audience. Each letter has a personal salutation. Some carry a short, handwritten personal note from the partner responsible for the client – particularly in those instances where the intended recipient is known.

Over the next week there is an initial high response, but this dips quickly. The names of known clients who have not responded are circulated to the partners concerned. The partners ensure that someone known to the client gives the client a call. A call could go something like this:

Good morning George. How are things at Rockford?

Busy as usual, what about with you?

Similar. There are a lot of things happening on the legislative front and we're gearing up for the client demand that is sure to follow. In fact, to some extent that's the purpose of my call. You may recall I sent you an invitation to a seminar last week. We're inviting a number of our clients to attend this complimentary morning to give them a briefing on the new employment legislation and how that is likely to impact upon their businesses in the future.

Yes, I recall seeing it in my post. It looked interesting.

Well, I thought that rather than just leave it as a mailed invitation I'd give you a call and personalise our welcome.

That's very kind John. Now I know there was a reason why I didn't reply to your letter. What was that? . . . Ah! I think I know. Is this seminar in five weeks' time?

That's right, it is.

Then that's the reason. I'm in our Geneva office all that week. Sorry, I should have come back to you.

No problem. I understand. I take it from your tone though that this is a subject you have an interest in.

I don't see how anyone can afford to turn a blind eye to the new laws. Whilst I don't pretend to understand the details of how we are going to re-package our contracts, I do know that failing to get it right could expose us to litigation and potential fines. The press has been full of that.

Most people are in a similar position. It's the detail of what they have to do and how they have to do it that is causing them concern – hence our seminar. Can I make a suggestion?

Sure.

Why don't we put a date in the diary when our senior employment partner and I can come out to meet with you – say the week after you get back from Geneva? I'll send you a copy of the slides used in the presentation just before we meet so that you at least have a gist of the key messages. Then we can take some time to discuss the situation at Rockwell. How does that sound?

Sounds good. Let me get my diary.

Not all telephone conversations end as fortuitously as this – but a few are similar. Also some 'waverers' make the decision to attend due to the extra personalisation of the invitation. The numbers swell to 40.

As in Firm A, the presenters in Firm B design the detail of the seminar.

An evening meeting is held two days before the seminar date. The presenters and the seven professional staff – all of whom either specialise in, or have a direct interest in, employment law, attend. They agree between themselves what time they will arrive at the venue. (All will be there before the possibility of the early-bird participant.) They agree how they will always have someone available to greet each guest after the guest has registered. They agree who will be personally responsible for each and every guest. They individually note down exactly what they want to raise with each guest for whom they are responsible and they lightheartedly practise a few opening lines to get a feel of 'what they're comfortable with'.

They also agree to 'own' a couple of opening questions that they will use at those times (e.g. coffee break) when they are in mingling mode. This will prevent any one participant enduring five conversations that begin with the words, 'So, what do you think so far?' The team also know that different openings to conversations lead to different conclusions and different information being exchanged. Again, lightheartedly they practise a few 'breaking off and moving on manoeuvres'.

The day before the seminar, three secretaries telephone each of the participants (or their secretaries) to ensure that they have received the joining instructions and to 'answer any last-minute questions about the day'. Four late cancellations are discovered through this exercise.

The day arrives and things go well. The hotel does its job well, all the Firm B professionals turn up on time, the meeting and greeting goes to plan and the seminar is professionally delivered. Of the 36 participants expected, 34 arrive. The Firm B professionals sit in on the seminar – particularly as this is the first time it has been run. It would look poor if any one of them were asked a question after the event and they were to give an answer which appeared to contradict the seminar messages. What is extremely valuable is observing the question-and-answer session. The professionals get a first-hand insight into how some of their clients are thinking due to the type of questions they pose to the presenters.

The morning is well delivered and managed – no better than Firm A's – but to the same standard. It has proven to be an extremely useful event for attendees.

Lunch follows, with the Firm B professionals ensuring that the participants do not accidentally sideline them. The professionals make every attempt at this stage to talk directly with their nominated guests. On numerous occasions we hear words to the effect of, 'Sounds like this is something we should talk about in a bit more detail. Obviously this is not the time and place. Should I drop you a line with a few thoughts when I get back to my office, then we can arrange to meet and discuss things somewhat further?'

When the last of the guests departs, the professionals return to the conference room for a 45-minute debrief. Taking one guest at a time, all useful information picked up in conversation is exchanged. It is interesting to note those professionals who have managed to circulate most successfully through the quantity and quality of information they are able to contribute at this point.

A secretary takes notes of key points to be updated on the database and records all agreed follow-up actions. All clients who gave up their time to attend will receive 'courtesy' follow-up letters. There are a number of other, more specific letters which individuals will construct within the next few days and there are numerous telephone calls to be made and appointments to be sorted out and kept.

It appears that the 34 guests could produce a total of sixteen meetings within the next few weeks. Thirteen of these meetings are to do with the seminar subject. Three are on other subjects that somehow arose in discussion. Of the sixteen meetings, two are with potential new clients, nine are with Valued Clients and five are with Key Clients. Winning the work associated with this impending change in legislation with just one Key Client will more than pay for all the time, money and effort put into organising, running and following up the seminar.

The professionals agree that it will be more realistic to expect the eventual results to be two or three times better than this – not taking into account the two prospective clients.

Making marketing work

Whilst the boundary between a Capability Marketing activity and a Contact Marketing activity may be sometimes a little hazy, there is no doubt in our definitions where these two seminar events fall in our pyramid. Firm B turned a Capability Marketing activity into a well-managed Contact Marketing activity. Firm A had a Capability Marketing activity – full stop. Some may want to debate this. After all, didn't Firm A's professionals also have contact with their clients? Not by our definition they didn't.

The two firms carried out one part of this exercise in a very similar fashion – the presentation. There was no discernible difference between the two: they were both good. However, in the case of Firm A the seminar proved to be a marketing cost whilst Firm B made a marketing investment.

Any Capability Marketing exercises, designed to persuade our clients that we have skills and capabilities outside of those they are currently aware of, will be far more effective if we can successfully seek ways to 'turbo charge' them by supporting them with Contact Marketing. The essence of Contact Marketing lies in engaging our professional staff in real dialogue with clients over real issues. This is why those firms that have found a successful formula for business breakfasts and themed lunches find these exercises so valuable. The success formula for both these events involves small, selected groups of personally invited participants, a topic of high interest to all attending, some expert and highly valued input (not necessarily provided by the host firm) and a group of selected, well-informed and well-prepared professionals who can continue the discussion with their guests.

Even Corporate Marketing activities can be turned into Capability and Contact Marketing opportunities. Take the example of sponsoring a local Business Club. To keep this as a Corporate Marketing activity we do what many organisations do: we send a junior member of staff to the Business Club meeting venue a few hours before starting time and have him arrange the strategic positioning of our company flag and the layout of the company brochures. If they are available, we will try to get a couple of staff along on the day to shake a few hands and demonstrate our commitment. To show that we are real corporate citizens, we will pick up the drinks bill after the event.

Turning this into a Capability Marketing exercise is not too difficult – it just takes a little effort. We have to be prepared to work with the Business Club committee – perhaps even become a member. We need to find out what the members of the club would find really interesting and valuable if they were going to give up either their business or personal time. Next, we need to agree with the committee which of the Business Club meetings we can take prime responsibility for organising. Clearly we are seeking to be the organiser of those meetings where our firm has strong expertise and a very powerful message.

The detailed organisation of the event from this point may not be dissimilar to that of Firm B in our earlier example. However, we should always look outside our own firm for presenters who can support our message. There is kudos in being able to attract known business personalities to an event we are running – not to mention the benefit of increasing the attendance. Additionally though, we must always leave a slot where one of our people gives our firm's input on the subject.

At the end of the presentation part of the Business Club meeting we can offer to send a copy of the slides to anyone who gives us his or her business card. This provides us with a later opportunity to make contact to check if the copy slides arrived and if the person has any questions on any element of the subject. Quite clearly we will have sufficient qualified and interested professional staff on hand on the day in question to manage the one-on-one discussions which occur over the wine and cheese which follows.

The organisation and presentation of a topical and valuable subject where we demonstrate we have capability and can add value to our clients' (and potential clients') thinking is turning a Corporate Marketing activity into a useful Capability Marketing exercise. The attempts to also initiate dialogue then progress us one stage further into Contact Marketing.

So will our clients co-operate?

We are hearing more frequently that professional firms are finding it difficult to attract the desired quantity and quality of people along to their marketing events. Professionals tell us there are two reasons for this. The first is that there are more and more people carrying out these events – seminars, round tables, business breakfasts and so on. Second, it appears that senior people are less likely to volunteer their attendance at such events.

There is little one can do to stop the competition from putting on their own marketing events. However, the question about the reduction in the number of 'movers and shakers' prepared to attend is an interesting one. The question, however, has a simple answer. Senior people in business have not restricted their attendance time at events run by professional firms for no apparent reason. There is a very simple reason. These senior business people concluded that, given the evidence of their experience, they were not getting value for the time they were investing.

In our scenarios earlier in this chapter we made some assumptions. In the Firm A/Firm B situation we took for granted that the subject chosen for the seminar was topical and of interest to key people within client firms. We also wrote in our story that the content and delivery of the seminar resulted in clients leaving after lunch feeling that the exercise had been either useful or extremely useful. We made similar assumptions in our Business Club illustration.

If we return to David Maister's conclusions about the effectiveness of marketing activities from the client's perspective, we will recall that for the activity to be effective, the client had to feel that she had gained something from it – some form of added value. In situations where people have their expectations of added value unfulfilled, they quickly decide not to repeat the experience. Also, word spreads quickly. If one director from a business attends a function he finds of low value, he is unlikely to keep this a secret.

In all our time in working with professional firms we cannot recall one instance where someone senior in a firm has said, 'We run seminars and presentations for our clients but they are poor.' We may be told that these events are good, very good or even excellent, but poor – never. But what is 'good'?

As people who earn their living from presenting daily to groups of all sizes, the authors could be accused of trying to set the bar too high. It could be argued that it is unrealistic to expect every technically expert person to also be a presenter of professional quality.

It is not professionals who have to be convinced about this view: it is their clients.

When managing directors and other senior people within businesses tell us of events run by professional firms where 'It started late', '. . . ran over time . . .', '. . . was clearly not rehearsed or practised . . .', '. . . the main speaker could have bored for England . . .', '. . . there was not one interesting presenter out of six . . .', '. . . there were constant technical breakdowns that the speaker had no idea how to sort out . . .',

'. . . the best bit was when the chairman fell off the stage!', we think there may be reason to question the real quality of some events that are run for clients.

Also, we must remember our audience. The type of people we are trying to attract may go to watch a play put on by their local amateur dramatic society, but mostly they are the sort of people who will pay to attend West End productions. One thing's for sure: they're astute enough to know the difference between the two. This raises the question: what do we do when our expert is not our best presenter – and no one on this earth is going to convert him into an excellent presenter? The short answer is that he should not carry out the presentation. Clearly the presenter must have some knowledge of the subject: the more, the better. We should recruit a good presenter with a reasonable knowledge of the subject to carry out most of the delivery and break the delivery at pre-determined points and invite questions from the participants. The subject-matter expert can field the questions. On an arranged signal the expert hands back to the presenter and the presentation moves ahead.

Are we making the quality of presentation and delivery too much of an issue? Isn't the message more important than the way it is delivered? In theory, yes; in the real world, no. The poor presenter with the most important of messages begins to lose his audience quickly. They begin to fidget. They have to work hard at listening. They find their minds beginning to wander. They start to tune in and tune out. Before long they are hardly listening and they are deriving very little value from the valuable messages which the presenter is delivering.

It is rare in our experience to hear of a professional firm putting a speaker forward at a seminar, conference or workshop who is not entirely technically capable of addressing the subject matter in question. The issue to be resolved is more about delivery than content.

A checklist for the ideal marketing activity aimed at clients

❑   The activity will involve exposing our existing clients to a capability that many of them will not associate closely with our firm.

❑   The activity or event will be aimed at clearly demonstrating our capability in this arena to our clients.

❑   The event will be managed in such a way that we turn it from a pure Capability Marketing exercise into a Contact Marketing exercise.

❑   The activity will inform and educate our clients. They will not feel they have been 'sold to'. They will leave our presence feeling they have received real value for the time they have invested. They will not leave feeling that we have omitted important answers in order to use these for fee-earning opportunities.

❑   The delivery and presentation of the event will be as professional as the quality of the message.

Using the Internet and the World Wide Web

The current situation

In the basket of marketing tools the Internet and the World Wide Web are new additions. Business websites have become increasingly common. Today most websites for professional services firms take the form of Corporate Marketing. We can discover on them the core values of the firm, where all the firm's offices are located and the types of work in which the firm is involved.

Such a website is like an electronic corporate brochure – a Corporate Marketing activity. The aim of many websites, however, is to have visitors return time after time. If a client or prospective client feels there is value in continually communicating with us electronically then it is not unreasonable to assume that many of these visitors will be more amenable at some stage to opening a face-to-face dialogue.

Website experts have been advising for years that sites need to be refreshed. If a visitor returns to a site on two or three occasions and finds no further value, then that person is unlikely to ever return again.

Let us consider the website in the light of three fundamental aspects of marketing professional firms:

1. Clients rate marketing activities that provide them with added value.
2. Our aim should be to demonstrate capability in our marketing.
3. We should aim to turn any Capability Marketing exercise into a Contact Marketing activity.

With these three criteria as drivers, the shape of future website design for the most astute professional firms is already mapped out.

The future

Websites must become more information-rich. This information must not just be about who has joined the firm recently and which other firms have been acquired in the last year; the information has to be of value to clients and should contain enough real detail to prove (not make claims about) the firm's capabilities in those areas of its business where it seeks to expand its franchise.

Clearly, if the site is to appeal to clients time after time, then it has to be refreshed continually. We believe that it will not be long before the leading professional services sites are updated daily. The aim is to get clients into the habit of thinking (for instance), 'If this new withholding tax rule does come into being, it is bound to have an effect on us. I wonder what Fox Lambourn & Jones have to say about it?'

A few keystrokes later the client has a considered overview and opinion on the new rules. This is extremely useful to the client, who may have her question answered. In many cases however, this information may give rise to the client telephoning for additional detail. The dialogue has then begun.

In addition to having an up-to-date, information-rich website, the Internet can be used in other ways to market our services and develop relationships with our clients.

We could construct an extranet, which is an extension of the concept of an intranet.

The people who have access to an intranet usually all work for the firm. Some of the larger professional services firms have built their own intranets. These are packed with information that could be valuable to people across the firm. Professionals' CVs are available, we can find out what work we have done for clients in other locations, we can find out who knows whom in prospective clients, and so on. Most would agree these are an invaluable way of sharing information firm-wide.

An extranet goes one step further. The extranet invites external parties to have access to shared information. Our clients are an obvious target for inclusion as part of our extranet audience. Clearly the information we make available on an extranet will, in the main, be different from that available on our intranet. Much intranet information is confidential and is also probably of little interest to our clients.

The concept is that any person or company can have access to our public website, but only our clients can have access to our extranet. The possibilities are endless from this point. For an organisation to continue to benefit from access to our extranet, they must continue as clients. If, after a certain length of time, work ceases to flow, then the free access to electronically provided information ceases.

There can also be different levels of access allowed to different clients. For instance, Valued Clients may have one level of access, Key Clients have another level and Crown Jewels Clients the highest level. When clients log on to our extranet we will able to track who has shown interest in what subject – potentially extremely valuable information.

Benefits

One of the benefits of electronic dialogue is that it can build a dependency which has mutual benefits for both supplier and customer. In the mid-1980s we ran seminars where one of the examples of achieving customer lock-in was the 'SKF story'. SKF, the Swedish-based bearings manufacturer, was an electronic pioneer, voluntarily providing its major auto manufacturing customers with direct electronic access to inventory levels at all its manufacturing sites across Europe.

This had benefits for both sides. First, automobile manufacturers were unlikely to experience the frustration and disruption caused when ordering a type of bearing only to find out that SKF were out of stock. Second, by keeping a weather eye on the stock levels of the bearing types for which they had greatest requirement, the auto manufacturers could time the placing of their orders more accurately. This was an early movement toward Just-In-Time manufacturing and away from Just-In-Case stockholding. The electronic tie-up increased SKF's sales and reduced the auto manufacturers' working capital requirement.

Two morals can be drawn from this story. The first point about mutual benefit has already been made. The second is that, whilst this may have been a revolutionary development in 1984, the story lost its impact a long time ago. Electronic 'discussion' between manufacturers and component suppliers is the norm, not the exception.

The 'threat' of the Internet

Above all, the Internet is a source of information. The 'products' provided by professional firms consist mainly of knowledge and expertise. Put these two concepts side by side and it is obvious that any firm that believes it has paid its electronic dues by investing in a static Corporate Marketing website will sooner, rather than later, be forced to play catch-up.

Many professionals we have spoken with are very uneasy about freely available information on the Internet. They see this as potentially undermining the services of professionals who, in the past, have charged fees for dispensing this knowledge. These same people are often also unhappy about giving 'too much' of value to clients in Capability Marketing activities. Their thinking is, 'If we give them too much information, they will go away and do it themselves.'

We have four responses to this thinking.

First, there will always be a small minority of people who will want to take our knowledge and not pay for it. They exist today. They are the clients and prospective clients who ask for proposals that not only spell out what we intend to do but how we intend to do it – in detail. They ask six other firms for the same. Their intent is dishonest. Given that we identify such behaviour, it is our choice if we wish to pursue work with these organisations.

Second, the majority of people in business want to focus on their business, not on trying to develop expertise in accountancy, surveying, law or systems consultancy. Providing them with information of value to them and to their business does not automatically mean that they will want to become pseudo-experts in our field of work: they probably have neither the time, energy nor inclination.

Third, we have to expect the world to change – and to change rapidly. Areas of work that we guard jealously today may become common public expertise in future. Take printing for instance. It was not long ago that if we wished to print a company newsletter we would write up the text and hand the whole job over to a printer. Some years ago desktop publishing (DTP) became the vogue. Specially trained people within our firm could use DTP packages so much of the layout and design work could be done in-house.

Time has marched on and now much of what was included in a DTP software package is now readily available in the office software packages that are loaded on to most PCs. Tens of thousands of secretaries can do work that was once restricted to a relatively small number of craftsmen, many of whom had served a formal apprenticeship to learn their trade. There is no point in trying to fight the tide of change.

There may well be some types of work and advice which will be provided in 'non-traditional' ways in the future. However, there will always be new opportunities to replace lost fee income streams, and we must be on the look-out for these.

The final reason for making the Internet a key part of our future marketing and client interface is that in the long run we will be forced to. Imagine a bearings manufacturer in the twenty-first century telling Ford that it was not prepared to do business and exchange information electronically. It is not a case of *if* we choose to use the Internet to market our firms; it is only a choice of *when* and *to what extent*. Will we lead or will we follow?

Contact Marketing over the Internet

Up to this point it may appear that electronic contact is a Capability Marketing activity. Whilst our clients benefit from accessing information which we publish and we can build our image of credibility in a particular practice area, there is no real dialogue.

Again, this is changing. Neural network software allows clients who have access to our extranet to ask us questions electronically. A client may wish to ask the question, 'What are the key factors I need to consider if I want to recruit staff from countries outside the EU?' The question is typed in using plain English. Sitting behind our extranet is a database that we are happy in allowing our clients to access. Neural network software is extremely clever. It accesses the information from wherever it lies within our database and brings the answers up on-screen. Not only that, the more the software is used and the more questions it is asked, the cleverer it becomes. The program 'learns' each time it is asked another question.

We are now moving well away from a 'dumb' Corporate Marketing website into the realms of an interactive Contact Marketing extranet. There is no science fiction here: all of this technology is available today, and some of it has been available for some time.

The Internet as a source of fee income

So far we have considered a website or an extranet as a form of marketing tool. It is possible, of course, to take this one stage further and turn the marketing tool into a form of revenue generation. This has been done for some years in parts of the IT industry.

As a customer of (say) a leading graphics software company, I can buy various levels of support. Whilst I can use a telephone hotline, most support is provided by direct Internet access to the software manufacturer.

At the highest level of support I have direct access to the software development engineers who can help me to reconfigure the package. It is possible that between my ideas at an application level and the resources of the HQ software engineers, we may develop an entirely new generation of product – totally tailored to my specific application needs. I gain great value for the money I have invested in the support package, and in this example the manufacturer may have also have had a positive result.

It is only a small step from allowing our clients to access parts of our knowledge database freely, to charging them for access – or for certain types of knowledge or access. Potentially the information resulting from the question about recruiting people from outside the EU could have been charged for.

It is too early to predict in detail how professional firms will use the Internet in the future – will it purely be a marketing tool or will it be a source of revenue? Our hunch is that it will be both. We feel that if firms seek to charge for every piece of information their clients take from their website or extranet, these clients will stop coming back in any quantity. Yet to 'give the entire shop away' would make little commercial sense. A balance of value-added information but with a premium paid for those things that constitute advice would appear to be the ideal aim.

Professional firms have a lot to learn about leveraging their use of the Internet, but they will undoubtedly learn very quickly. They have to.

FIRST STEPS

1. Find out from your clients what 'image' they have of your firm – what words come into their head when the name of your firm is mentioned. Find out where they see your firm as having expertise, and where not. Make sure that this information is gained in such a way that it is accurate and honest.

2. Take a good look at the promotional activities you are carrying out. Are they designed to prove to your clients your capability in areas you wish to promote and which would be of interest to them? Do your clients feel they get real value from every one?

3. Compare your marketing activities to the 'Firm B scenario' in this chapter. Decide which new ideas would be useful to implement, and plan to include them in the design and management of your next event.

Chapter 5 **Selling to Clients**

'The best source of new work is our existing client base.' This statement has been made countless times by partners with an interest in new business development – and the statement is true, particularly if we replace the word 'client' with the words 'Key Client'. In Chapter 2 many of the ways we used to define Key Clients were to do with the volume and profitability of work these clients are providing today or the volume and profitability they are capable of generating in the future.

In this chapter we will concern ourselves with selling more of our current capability to existing clients. We will assume that the work we are trying to sell can either be conducted by our practice area or will be managed by our practice area. In Chapter 6 we will specifically focus on the situation where our selling attempts involve trying to introduce other parts of our firm.

We address the following in this chapter:

- How to spot opportunities for work.
- Developing new products for clients.
- Selling additional products to clients – and how to differentiate between real opportunities and phantom opportunities.
- How to manage the selling opportunity – particularly in a competitive situation.

SPOTTING OPPORTUNITIES

The problem

'I don't understand it. My junior people are on the client's premises for weeks at a time. They have the opportunity to delve into anything and everything. Yet it is unusual for them to find one additional opportunity for work. When I spend time with the client, I constantly see ways in which we can help them further. Why is that? Can you train my people to be better?'

This is a cry for help we have heard on numerous occasions. Can we help? Partially. Some of the solution lies in skills we can enhance, but a great deal of the answer rests with the person who has expressed the problem.

Analysing the problem

Why are these people working on the client's site? The most common answers are:

- They need information that is most easily accessed by being on the client's premises.
- They are carrying out some work (for instance implementing a new system) which physically exists on the client's premises.

The first of these answers needs to be qualified by two further questions:

- How much of this information do our people access from people within the client and how much do they access from physical sources (paper files, computer records, etc.)?
- When accessing information from people, how much of this dialogue is with 'technical' people (who tend to have a narrow view of their area of expertise) and how much is with managerial people (who have a wider vision)?

Reasons for the problem

Perhaps by posing these questions some parts of the answer start to emerge. Take (for instance) the role of a newly qualified accountant working on an audit team. Even though many audit firms are trying to change the focus of the audit from substantive and compliance auditing to assessing business risk, there is still a lot of detailed legwork which is carried out by the more junior people on the team. Our clients describe how their auditors lock themselves away in an office for days or weeks at a time, emerging only occasionally to request another file.

It is hardly surprising that people who carry out this type of work fail to find opportunities. They have a process to carry out. They put their heads down and work away at this process. Their horizon is hardly likely to extend beyond the door of the office. Our suggestion is not to drop this type of work. We are not qualified to give any view on what should and should not be included in an audit or to make comment on the way it is conducted. However, we should not have unreasonable expectations of people whose role is purely technical and whose interface is almost solely with a client's records. What about people from our team who *do* have the opportunity to speak with people from within the client's organisation – and not just to technical people about technical detail? Can they spot an opportunity if it appears?

Let us step back and consider why a client uses professionals at all. There are a few services that a client *has* to buy: the audit is one. There is a legal requirement for companies to have their accounts audited. These types of services are in the minority; the majority are services that the client has a wish to undertake but does not have the internal capability (or desire) to execute. For example, a business wishing to sell one of its divisions could search the marketplace for a suitable buyer, but many companies will choose to use the services of a corporate finance specialist to assist them in this process.

The client considers that the business benefits gained from the use of professional support are greater than the costs associated with using professional input. In many instances the decision to use professional support is a 'no brainer'. In other words, the business benefits outweigh the likely costs many times over.

So what is a definition of an opportunity? An opportunity is an opening for professional advice where it is likely that the advice provided can assist the client with substantial business benefits that will outweigh any costs associated with the execution of the professional help.

And what are the most influential business benefits for any individual client? This depends on what the client is trying to achieve.

- Client A's game plan could be to gain market share through diversification of its existing product portfolio.
- Client B may have the same objective of gaining market share but through stripping out costs from its business and being able to offer the lowest cost product.
- Client C may be aiming for the same target but trying to achieve this through increasing demand for a small number of core products and thereby reaping the benefits of lower unit costs of production.
- Client D could be pursuing an acquisition strategy.
- Client E could be interested in profit rather than market share.

An opportunity starts as an idea in someone's mind – in our case, in the mind of a professional who is working with a client. If the professional sees an opening which he can directly relate to the objectives and chosen strategy of the client organisation, two things will happen:

1. He will recognise the opportunity.
2. He should feel confident enough to pursue the opportunity, raising it either with his own people or directly with the client.

Too many professionals do not know the business objectives of the clients with whom they work. They do not understand the chosen strategies of their clients. Even if the strategies were explained to them they would not understand the context of these strategies because they do not understand the dynamics of the sector in which the client works.

How do we come to make this claim? In our discussions with professionals about their personal development, the one area in which they consistently admit they have a knowledge shortfall and where they would like input, is in the area of sector-specific knowledge. This even happens with some people who are promoted by their firms as sector-focused specialists. A team we worked with who spent their entire lives working with clients in the banking sector perceived their greatest learning need to be in the area of understanding the client's business and the client's sector.

Sadly for us, this is not our area of training expertise. However, it is training that can quite easily be constructed and provided through a variety of learning sources. We would suggest to our partner, who bemoaned the capability of his junior people, to test how much real understanding his people have of their clients and their marketplaces. If, as we suspect, their knowledge is inadequate then let us, for a moment, put ourselves in the shoes of one of these people.

Would we want to have an in-depth discussion with a (senior) manager within a client's business if we knew that our naïvety and lack of in-depth understanding would be demonstrated very quickly? Would we have the temerity to suggest an idea (let alone to actively sell it) if we were completely uncertain where it fitted within the client's thinking and the client's strategy? The answers are obvious. We would probably keep our heads down and retire to the office where we have worked for the last few days and be seen to have performed a sound piece of technical work.

The solution

Selling skills training is not the first step in putting our people in position to spot opportunities. The first step is give them the knowledge, understanding and confidence about the client's business so that they can recognise how something they perceive as an opportunity can fit into, and support, the client's business direction. Given this starting point, skills development and an understanding of effective opportunity management have a firm foundation on which to build.

DEVELOPING NEW PRODUCTS

Scenario 1

'Come in and meet John. John and his team are developing our new range of products for the future. They are working on some really exciting ideas.'

The introducer is clearly very proud of his product development team. The firm is really commercial now. It refers to 'products' and not 'services'. This shows that there is confidence that the firm can really capture the essence of a service, wrap it up, badge it, promote it and sell it – just like real marketeers.

A year later John and his team are back in the front line delivering work to clients. Few products materialised. Those that did materialise received very little real support from the firm's professional staff and even less from the clients to whom they were introduced. The product development team champion has moved on to champion some other marketing initiative.

The fundamental shortcoming

This scenario is not generated from our imaginations. We have experienced similar situations in our work in all manner of professional services firms – but consultancies in particular seem to have phases of product development focus. In the situation above, the person in control of events believed he was doing the right thing: he was being proactive in managing that particular aspect of marketing activity known as product development.

There is a fundamental problem with this scenario – it is conducted at a distance from the client.

New product development – Walkman versus V-tec

There are two ways to develop new products:

1. Create a product that no one knows they have a need for, but when it is released, everyone suddenly demands. This gives us a unique product and the potential for high market share and profitability. We will call this the Sony Walkman method. When Sony originally launched the Walkman it was one of scores of new electronic products released onto the Japanese market. There was no market research or shrewd marketing strategy behind it. It was an idea that someone in a product development group had dreamed up because it was technically possible. It went on to become a huge worldwide success.

2. Create a product for which we know there is some demand because we have already tested the product with other clients and we know that it has an application and that it works. We will call this the V-tec method. When turbo chargers were banned from Formula One racing, racing teams were looking for ways to generate more power from normally aspirated engines. Honda developed V-tec technology. This technology enabled racing engines to deliver more power right through the rev. range. Having a proven concept, Honda then took the next step by introducing this technology to a host of other customers who also valued power throughout the rev. range – the sporty motorist. Put together a proven concept and a ready market and the result is reassuringly certain. Those who copy and follow in the footsteps of the original product developers demonstrate the proof of the product's market value.

V-tec product development is not as exciting as Walkman product development. With Walkman development the market is shocked and delighted by an answer to a question it had not even begun to compose. The accolades from this type of forward thinking are mind-blowing.

With V-tec development, however, the world watches and the expansion of the product concept is probably obvious to all. It is hard to conceive that Ford were not fully aware that Honda were introducing V-tec engines to their passenger car range.

Walkman product development has one major shortcoming. When trying to generate a product which will pre-empt people's perceived needs, one has to be prepared to launch a hundred failures. The great product developers realise this. 3M encourages its product development people to take risks and to pursue totally new avenues – knowing that many of these will lead nowhere. They budget to spend multiple millions of development dollars on product 'failures'. That is fine for 3M, and over the years they have found ways of living with, and managing, this huge uncertainty of how to develop new winning products.

We do not see this style of new product development management fitting with many professional services firms that we have worked with over the years. Yet we still find people taken out of the client interface and put into an office with the designation of 'product development team'. A Walkman attempt in a totally wrong environment. It is not part of the firm's thinking that this group of talented people may produce three years of 'failures' before they have a success. Somehow this group of people is charged with having to produce success right away. 3M cannot guarantee this from their people, but accountant Jones and his team have this burden to carry.

We believe in V-tec product development.

There is a question posed by Ries and Trout in their book *Marketing Warfare*. They ask what should come first – strategy or tactics. The answer we receive when we pose this question related to product development is always the same. It is strategy of course.

Ries and Trout go on to illustrate that the vast number of product successes occur through a less theoretically perfect route. Typical of this is the situation where someone, somewhere, has a local success with something they have developed for a particular application. They realise that their product or solution has a wider application. They sell it to a few more customers. Local demand grows. They press head office with their concept. Someone perceptive within head office recognises the potential of the product development. Within a period of time a strategy is formulated to deliver the new product to a recognised market sector.

Years later, when the company chairman writes his memoirs, he recounts the excellent strategy he and his team formulated when they introduced product X. This becomes lore and it is only the determined researcher who digs deep enough to discover that the strategic plan was based on the foundations of proven tactical successes.

Our experience leads us to support this conclusion wholeheartedly. Whilst not wishing to denigrate creativity, we find little evidence that the senior management team of a business who spend three days away carrying out 'blue sky thinking' really do much to affect a business's real strategy. Sound, successful strategy is based on what works in the real world and, in relation to new product development, what is proven to sell in the real world.

Our messages on new product development are:

- We should work very closely with our clients, seeking to deliver *exactly* what they want.
- In seeking to deliver exactly what our clients want we should tailor and adapt our standard products and services.
- We should listen to a client's 'unreasonable' demands and try to find new ways to accommodate these. (In our own business some of our best product developments have come via this route.)
- We should recognise when we have reconfigured our product to such an extent that we have created something new – and workable.
- We should then seek to talk to other similar clients to see if this application is a one-off or is replicable.
- If the need exists elsewhere we should seek to refine and develop the product further and introduce a proven concept to a ready market.

SELLING PRODUCTS

Scenario 2

'OK, we need to plan how we are going to conduct this meeting with the client. This is a real opportunity for us because the client's three main people will all be there. What products are we are going to try to sell?'

The speaker feels good about his gathering. He has the four people from the Client Service Team present, all representing their individual parts of the firm. This get-together is happening three days before the meeting with the client – not in the taxi, as so often happens. Lots of discussion follows – with all sorts of options put on the table and debated. An agreement is reached and a 'batting order' of priority established.

At the meeting with the client there is just not the right opportunity to open up the selling discussion. The client pulls the meeting this way and that and, apart from five minutes at the end where the Client Service Team leader hurriedly throws out a few suggestions, the chance to introduce new products passes by.

Perceptions about selling

It is still a common perception that selling is about 'pitching' or 'presenting'. Many professionals see selling as the process of impressing a client with services and capabilities that they have not yet had the opportunity of taking from us. Therefore, planning to sell is all about thinking about what we believe fits the client's organisation and then, at the first opportunity, pitching in and 'selling' our concept.

We have witnessed some extraordinary conclusions being drawn when professionals have gathered together (as in Scenario 2 above) to consider what products, services and capabilities could fit their shared client. These conclusions could be based on

- what other similar clients appear to be doing;
- what someone believes will be good for the client;
- information from dubious sources;
- information clearly past its sell-by date;
- opinions posing as facts;
- hunches.

The whole approach typified in Scenario 2 suffers from the same shortcoming as the product development situation in Scenario 1 – it is removed from the critical input source – the client.

THE PACES MODEL WHEN SELLING TO EXISTING CLIENTS

In our book *Creating New Clients* we devoted a large section of the publication to the skills and processes of selling. In that book the focus was on how we sell to people who have never used our services previously. We introduced a model – the PACES model.

P Position ourselves and our organisation.

A Ascertain in detail the client's situation and requirements.

C Confirm to the client our understanding of their situation and requirements.

E Explain or explore a way forward.

S Seek commitment to the suggested way forward.

In conducting the A and C part of a selling meeting we introduced the funnel process. The funnel is a way of structuring questions so that each question follows logically the answer that precedes it. In *Creating New Clients* we also examined how we ensure that we enter a meeting armed with the right 'funnel opening' questions. So how does selling to existing clients differ in structure from selling to prospective clients?

Positioning

It could be argued that we could dispense with this part of the selling process. After all, if the client has been dealing with us for ten years she knows who I am and she believes in our firm's (and my personal) credibility, competence and compatibility – all those things that *Creating New Clients* says we should be trying to prove to a new contact.

If we are tempted to ignore this part of the selling process, let us refer back to the previous chapter. Our strength is our weakness. Because we are positioned in the client's mind as experts in the field in which she has used us in the past, she probably finds it difficult to position us in any other way. And remember, we are trying to sell her a new product, a new capability – something she has never experienced from us in the past.

Taking some time to position (or re-position) is extremely important, and by itself is still unlikely to totally convince the client.

An example – the HR Consultancy, Scene 1

As an illustration, let us take a firm called the HR Consultancy. They have a client with whom they have worked for three years. Originally the consultancy was involved in a competitive bid for management development work. They won. In the early days of the relationship they were very concerned to deliver to the highest possible standard. They chose not to try to break out of this type of work until they had established an image of high competence and credibility in the execution of management development programmes. Over the last three years the consultancy has carried out training programmes which have been well received for both their relevance and practicality.

The client now positions the consultancy as 'our management trainers'. The consultancy, however, believes the time is right to seek new areas of work from the client. One of the avenues of work carried out by the consultancy is the development of appraisal systems. The consultants carrying out the training work have had constant anecdotal feedback on the poor state of repair of the current appraisal system. It appears to be out of date, badly flawed and difficult to use. This is 'bread and butter' work to the consultancy as a whole. Consultants who carry out management training for one client can often be found working on the development of appraisal processes for another.

We will eavesdrop on a meeting between the Client Service Team leader for the consultancy and the Human Resources Director of the client. Before the meeting the professional has sent an agenda. Most of the agenda points relate to current business, but the final point is entitled 'Additional areas of future support'.

Client:	*OK. That's all fine. We're very happy with the work you've done in the past, and the action plan to follow up the last course looks good. Your idea for preparing our managers better before the training looks excellent too. That just about ties everything up except for this last item, 'Additional areas of future support'. I have to say I am intrigued but I've remained patient up to this point to find out what this is about.*
Consultant:	I appreciate that – but like you I wanted to ensure that we closed off all the details of the work we're engaged in today before starting to look at other potential issues. Can I just check something? When we started the meeting we said a maximum of an hour and a half. I make it that we've still got about 35 minutes or so. If we find ourselves into something interesting here, do we still have that 35 minutes?
Client:	*Yes. At a push I can make it three-quarters of an hour, but then I have another meeting to attend.*
Consultant:	Fine. I'll make sure I don't stray over that time limit. Should I start?
Client:	*Please do.*
Consultant:	If we go back three years, we were invited to bid for your management training work. I recall at the time you said to me that an ex-colleague who had been particularly pleased with our work had referred our name to you.
Client:	*That's right, it was Jim Jardine at Thompsons. I understand you're still doing work for him.*
Consultant:	Jim had used us for management training as well – hence his referral. Since winning your management development contract we have been very focused on meeting your exact requirements – naturally enough – and not concerned at all about trying to introduce you to the wider capabilities of our firm.
Client:	*Such as?*
Consultant:	Well, our business was originally founded as a surrogate Human Resources Directorship. We provided the HR function to companies who realised they needed this type of support but who didn't want to go the whole distance and employ a full-time HR director or

manager. So our role could encompass any aspect of human resources work.

Client: *I didn't realise that.*

Consultant: As I recall, we mentioned it in passing in our presentation three years ago, but when you're looking for a training provider I guess that's not the sort of information that is going to make a great deal of impression.

Client: *No, I don't recall that.*

Consultant: We still provide this service to some of the smaller clients with whom we deal. It provides excellent hands-on opportunities to deal with real issues and real people. Depending on the situation, we can be asked to recruit people, construct induction programmes, advise on remuneration programmes and packages, supervise disciplinary situations, construct appraisal processes, train people in carrying these processes out, devise training programmes, and, as you are aware, deliver these programmes.

More of our work in recent years has been with larger clients who do not require a surrogate HR manager. Typically, these clients have initially employed us to carry out projects that very often involve only one aspect of our capability. Our relationship with you is not untypical. You use us to design and deliver management training because that is a gap you perceived three years ago and you did not have people within the business capable of conducting this level of training.

In the same way that you have volunteered to be a reference point for our capabilities as management developers, we equally have other clients who act as referees for our capabilities in other aspects of HR work.

Client: *That's interesting. So do you think there are other areas where you can help us? I sense that is the direction in which we are going.*

Consultant: It would be somewhat presumptuous for me to claim that, but there is one area I would like to explore with you if I may. That is the subject of your appraisal system.

At this point the meeting can begin to focus on the subject which the professional has selected. However, the professional has taken the time to give some background and assurances that this area of work is not alien to his firm's skill-set. We must not assume that the client understands our firm's positioning in the way we do. She will have a very distinct picture – but that picture could be far removed from the image we understand.

At the right time, positioning (or re-positioning) of the firm is an essential opening element to the selling process.

A and C before E and S

This was put forward in *Creating New Clients* as the fundamental order for the selling process. The concept is extremely simple. First of all we need to understand the client's situation and requirements (A), then check our understanding through summarising and reflecting (C), to make sure that we really have got the correct picture, as perceived by the client, in full.

Then we can go on to discuss and present potential solutions (E). If our ideas are on the mark we can then seek agreement to a way forward (S). Understand the problem, then present a solution. Nothing earth-shattering in that methodology, but as we discussed in *Creating New Clients*, there are many reasons why professionals 'break the rules' and find their selling efforts poorly rewarded.

So why should this process only apply to prospective clients? Is there an argument to say that we can dispense with this process when selling to existing clients? There is only one situation when we can dispense this order of events. This is the situation where we

- know the background 'business drivers' for the client's organisation and how our solution will fit with these;
- understand in total our client's requirement for the new product or capability that we intend to introduce and sell to her;
- understand how our expertise will fit in with the client's specific situation;
- know how our solution will improve what they are doing today and by how much;
- know how it will be received by – and how it will affect – all of the people who may be involved in some way in reaching the decision to use our new product;
- know the bases of decision of all of the people who may become involved in the decision to use the new product we intend to introduce to our client. We not only understand the rational 'needs', we also have a good feel for the emotional 'wants' of the people involved;
- know that the client's budget means they can afford our solution;
- understand fully the process the client will go through to consider our solution;
- know we don't have to bother about any specific positioning to overcome a competitor's offering. If there are competitors, we know who they are and how to position ourselves to advantage against them.

So, given positive answers to all the above points, we can accurately position our pitch, turn up and deliver our selling arguments. We have a good chance of success.

Reality and experience tell us that we probably have little understanding of the above issues in relation to a new product that we would ideally like to sell to an existing client. We have hunches, we have opinions, we may think we know. Guesses, however, are no basis for a successful selling approach. The answers to all of the above points – factors that will determine the success of our selling approach – lie with people who populate our client's organisation. To be successful in selling new products to our clients, we have to base our approach upon sound data. Prospective clients or existing clients, it makes no difference. It is still A and C before E and S.

Ascertaining the client's requirements and confirming our understanding – differentiating between real and 'phantom' opportunities

A few years ago, on a training programme we were running for one of our consultancy clients, one of the participants (a bright, eager young man) told us

> When I'm working on a client's site, I don't have a problem spotting things we could provide them with. The problem seems to be that when I try to sell the idea to someone within the client, they're not interested. Could it be that because I have a hammer, everything looks like a nail?

We had come across this problem scores of times previously. We had never heard the problem so succinctly expressed. The nub of this problem is that too often professionals embark on selling a solution before the client realises she has an opportunity to be exploited or a problem to be solved. The old rule of A and C before E and S (in the PACES process) has been broken.

Sometimes professionals argue with our diagnosis. They say things like, 'I asked the client about the situation. There was a very clear need. There must be another explanation why the client was not interested. Either that or the client is deliberately being perverse.' Our experience in working with professionals leads us to conclude that there can be huge variation in the quality of understanding that professionals develop about the needs and wants of their clients. There are two reasons for this.

1. The professional is not inquisitive. There could be all sorts of explanations for this, though we are constantly surprised by the ability of big firms in particular to take creative, inquisitive graduates and turn them into conformist, tunnel-visioned specialists within two or three years.

   Whatever the explanation for the lack of inquisitiveness, if the professional does not have the intrinsic interest in the client and the client's business, he will not have the motivation to really explore and understand the client's needs and wants. A superficial understanding is built up through association with the client. This superficial understanding acts as the basis for selling attempts. Unsurprisingly, many of these miss the mark.

2. The professional does not have a high enough level of skill to drill down and to really understand the client and her business.

   The skills are easily delineated. There are two – questioning and listening. So simple: so simple that many professionals believe that because they understand the concept then they must be quite good (if not exceptional) in the execution. After all, anyone can ask questions and listen.

   Unfortunately, real-life observation provides overwhelming evidence that this is not the case. Professionals very often confuse the development of skills with the accumulation of knowledge. A non-golfer can quickly learn the theory of playing golf. How to hold the club. How to address the ball. How to swing. How to follow through. It is all very easy. Simply put the videotape in the player, sit back for an hour and pay attention. Someone who has paid close attention could even answer questions on the subject.

It is obvious, however, that the armchair golfer will have little success when he steps onto that driving range for the first time. Watching the video will not have done him any harm, but equally it will have provided little real help. Playing golf is all about executing what is in our head, not simply about having information lodged in our brain.

It is the same with questioning and listening. The principles can be explained in minutes. Illustrations of good practice can be well demonstrated in under an hour. To be really good at implementing the skills requires training, feedback, coaching and ongoing practice – just like golf, or any other skill for that matter. The good news is that best practice is clearly defined and is 'learnable' for anyone who has the motivation.

By way of illustration, let us return to our Human Resources professional, speaking with his client and wanting to examine the subject of the client's appraisal process and system.

The HR Consultancy, Scene 2

Consultant: . . . there is one area I would like to explore with you if I may; that is the subject of your appraisal system.

Client: *What made you choose our appraisal system?*

Consultant: When we are running our management development workshops the subject often comes up – raised by your people. The feedback we get is that they understand what the process is for but they feel that the system today sometimes gets in the way of what they are trying to achieve – instead of facilitating it. What they are telling us is that the format and the process have been around for a long time and don't necessarily reflect the direction of the business today. They have to modify the way they use the process. They can't use it as it stands. Their feelings are that it may be time for a revamp and examination through fresh eyes. What do you think?

Client: *I can't ague too hard against those kinds of feelings. The system was put in place even before I arrived, and, with one thing and another taking precedence, it has never been re-visited or brought up to date. It never seems like the right time – even now.*

There we have it – a need. The appraisal system is outdated and no longer fit for use in its current state. The client has admitted it. Given that we have a need, the professional can now proceed with the E and S part of the PACES process. He can explain how his firm can help and seek commitment to a way ahead that will bring his firm a step closer to winning work in this new arena.

Consultant: I know we can help you with this. Do you remember a few minutes ago I told you that we constantly work on real-life implementation issues as well as providing training and development? Well, with regard to appraisal system development, let me tell you what we can do and how we can help your organisation. We have built up . . .

The consultant is now moving into real 'sell' mode.

Fifteen minutes later the client is definitely cool. She is not excited by this promise of a solution. She is telling the consultant, 'Put your ideas down on paper and I will consider them.' The consultant contemplates three hours writing a proposal. He envisions a client who is even less interested than she appears now, opening his proposal and glancing at it. He sees the proposal gathering dust at the bottom of the client's in-tray.

How did this happen when the client so obviously had a need? There was a definite nail to be hit. As soon as the hammer appeared, the nail seemed to lose its definition. Where did it all go wrong?

Let us go back to the dialogue. There was a hint there. Did you spot it first time through? This is much easier to do with the written word than the spoken word. The spoken word cannot be revisited – at least not with very much accuracy.

The HR Consultancy, Scene 3

Client: *. . . and with one thing and another taking precedence it has never been re-visited or brought up to date. It never seems like the right time – even now.*

We will give the consultant another chance.

Consultant: I'm interested in what you've just said – particularly the bit about 'even now'. What did you mean by that?

Client: *Totally off the record?*

Consultant: Sure.

Client: *Next Monday there will be an announcement of a total reorganisation. We are going over to a divisional structure. We are splitting into three trading businesses. You may have heard the rumours already.*

Consultant: I have. So what is the effect of this and how will this impact on the appraisals situation?

Client: *The different divisions will have different objectives. This means that people will be charged with doing new and different things. By definition one company-wide appraisal system will not fit all situations. There are many processes and systems that will have to be tailored to the new divisional requirements. and the appraisal process is one of them.*

Consultant: So this is something you will address, but when you do, there will be three projects and not one then?

Client: *That's right.*

Consultant: OK. Let me tell you how we can help you in the future with these projects . . .

Our consultant is off again into 'sell' mode. By listening to the client and unbundling what she said about, '. . . right time. Even now', he is not going to try and shove an untimely and ill-fitting solution upon his client. He has a broader understanding of the client's situation. He begins to position a solution aimed at three divisions with differing objectives. He positions the timing of this solution 'when the new organisation has settled down'.

Ten minutes later a client who is displaying signs of non-interest faces our consultant. How did this happen? The need is clear and the solution is tailored. It is positioned to account for the new structure and the future timescales.

We will give our consultant another attempt.

The HR Consultancy, Scene 4

Consultant: So this is something you will address, but when you do, there will be three projects and not one then?

Client: *That's right.*

Consultant: When you address the issue, who will be involved?

Client: *I want the new divisional directors to take ownership of this. I will provide whatever help I can, but I want them to drive it. When we get round to formally re-vamping the appraisal process I want to ensure it fits like a glove with the three new divisions. It will – if we get the involvement of the top operational people.*

Consultant: And when do you anticipate this will happen?

Client: *I can't see us making much of a move on it in the next ten months at least.*

No wonder the client was lukewarm to promises of help in the earlier scenes. Further qualification of the 'opportunity' shows it to be a medium- to long-term possibility at best. However, our consultant wants to qualify the situation further.

Consultant: Listening to your people it would seem, however, that the current situation is unsatisfactory. In trying to struggle on using a system that really doesn't fit, what impact do you think this is having?

Client: *Not much really. I've had several discussions with our management team on this subject. My stance is very simple. I know the process and the forms are outdated but there is no point in updating them until they can reflect the new divisional objectives – as I have said.*

My guidance to all our managers is to carry through the spirit of our appraisal process and use the current system and documentation as a rough guide. I want our managers to sit down with their people at least twice a year with the door shut. I want them to review their people's progress toward objectives, give them time to talk through where they are, what they do well, what they need to improve on, what their objectives are for the future, and what help and support they need to get there.

I've told them to use any parts of the current system which aid this type of discussion and to ignore the bits that get in the way. For the most part the managers have responded extremely well. Our people are very flexible and they seem to have taken the message on board. Of course they moan about the old system. I can easily understand the feedback your trainers must get. We will update the appraisal system one day – but in the light of the current situation it is not a high priority.

Consultant: So the appraisal system is an issue for the business. However, you do not perceive it as critical because, first, your people are, in the main, finding a way of working around the problem and, second, there is no point in addressing the situation until the new divisional structure is up and running. Have I got that right?

Client: *Spot on. I was afraid you were going to try to sell me some appraisal system design consultancy.*

The opportunity is fading fast. However, this is not all bad news. Given this position, the consultant is unlikely to wade in with an inappropriate, 'Let me tell you how we can help . . .', and be faced ten minutes later with polite refusals or unenthusiastic requests for 'something in writing'.

Real opportunities and 'phantoms'

The client perceives the need as very minor and something to be addressed only in the fullness of time. We have moved a long way. Our consultant originally believed there was a real burning need. One of the first things the client stated was '. . . it has never been re-visited or brought up to date'. It appeared as though the client had admitted there was an issue.

What the consultant failed to do in Scene 2 was to understand the perceived impact of the issue. In his latest attempt he has asked a type of question we hear all too rarely. *He asked the client's opinion regarding the impact of the issue.*

Clearly, given this situation, we long to hear the client describe how the problem is causing extreme demotivation, low work standards, unacceptably high staff turnover and over-budget recruitment costs. In an ideal world the client may also say that, faced with these problems, she is seeking help to find a fix for the offending appraisal process which is the root cause of all this misery!

The real issue, the issue as perceived by the client, could lie anywhere on a continuum between two extremes. At one end we have the outdated appraisal process causing extreme pain for the business; at the other it is a non-issue.

We will not find out where the 'opportunity' lies on this continuum by superimposing our values and perceptions onto the client. We have to ask the client. We have to make it explicit. We have to ask the question 'How much does this hurt?' or the question 'How much would you like to able to fully exploit this potential opportunity?'

When we have a client who replies 'It hurts a lot', or 'It's costing us money not being able to exploit the opportunity in the market', then we have a client who has reason to listen to what we may have to offer.

We can define the difference between a real opportunity and a phantom opportunity if we qualify it in this way. We can find out if we have discovered a real nail rather than something that looks like a nail.

Phantom opportunities exist because the professional believes the client has an issue that needs resolving but the client does not share this belief. Faced with this situation, most professionals try harder to convince the client there is an issue. In effect the professional is working hard to make the client understand she is wrong. One does not need a degree in psychology to realise this is unlikely to be a winning strategy.

Let us return to our consultant once again. At this point in the discussion, all of the doors appear to be closing. His initial perception of the appraisals issue does not match the Human Resources Director's current perception – and she will have a big say in the way forward on this subject.

The HR Consultancy, Scene 5

Often professionals are so focused on finding an angle to introduce their chosen subject that they fail to listen to the client. Our consultant has sat back, relaxed, focused, listened and made brief notes of key points raised by the client. The meeting could go forward as follows.

Client: *. . . I can easily understand the feedback your trainers must get. We will update the appraisal system one day – but in the light of the current situation it is not a high priority.*

Consultant: Can I take you back a few minutes. You said earlier something about having 'many processes and systems that will have to be tailored to the new divisional requirements' – the appraisal process being but one of them. What did you mean by that?

Client: *There will be some significant new practices required in the new regime. Line managers will become more accountable. In particular they will be much more responsible for day-to-day HR issues. They will have to manage the recruitment of their own people in future and run their own induction programmes tailored to their part of the business.*

> *We will still have a central HR function, but it is going to be scaled down. We can provide some help and guidance, but line managers are going to have to do these things for themselves.*

Consultant: Correct me if I'm wrong, but you seem to be scaling down your central HR function at the very time your line managers may need support to carry out new tasks?

Client: *No, you're not wrong. It's a very insightful comment. We've made the same point. However, the centre is insistent that if we go to a divisional structure there must be a large cut in all central functions. The cuts and the restructuring happen concurrently.*

Consultant: I sense that decision frustrates you.

Client: *It certainly does. I see the business reasons for autonomous divisions and lowered Head Office costs, but the whole thing could be achieved in a less high-risk way if only they would phase it.*

Consultant: So how will you manage to prepare your line managers with the right systems and the right skills to carry through their new responsibilities?

Client: *Now there we have a real problem. We cannot do it internally so we are going to have to look for outside assistance.*

Consultant: What would happen if, for some reason, you simply could not find any way of providing the right level or type of support to these line managers?

Client: *Some would battle through, but overall we would face huge problems in the future. Our business is based on hiring and training the best people. If we have a flawed recruitment process in any of the new divisions we risk . . .*

Our consultant has asked the telling question again. The client said, '. . . we have a real problem'. However, the consultant did not leave the discussion there. He then asked how much that problem would hurt if a solution could not be found. The answer that seemed to be shaping up was that this could be critical to the client's business.

Further qualification of the opportunity

There is a real opportunity here that needs to be further qualified. There is a mass of information that the consultant must gather before explaining or exploring a way forward for his firm to follow up the potential work. The consultant still needs to ask:

- How does the recruitment and induction programme work today?
- What is the role of the Central HR function in these tasks? What is the role of line management today?
- How is it envisaged to work in the future? What processes will the new divisions be asked to put in place?
- When will this handover of function happen?

- Which of the divisions will be most immediately impacted by the change, and why?
- What help and support will the slimmed-down Central HR function be able to provide in the future?
- What new or different skills and knowledge will line managers be required to have?
- In what areas is it believed that outside support can make the greatest contribution?
- In appointing outside advisers to help with this situation, how will the decision be made within the three different divisions? Who will be involved and at what stage will they become involved?
- If outside advisers are employed, what criteria will the people involved in making this choice use in order to reach their decision?
- What thought has been given to the funding required to support the line managers and the HR function, given this situation? Where will the money come from in the new structure to pay for advisers? Who will hold the budget? What is the budget? What would happen if a division saw a solution it really wanted, but it was slightly above the allocated budget or it was over an individual's signing-off limit?
- What would our current contact, the Human Resources Director, like to see as a solution? What would she like to get out of the relationship with a firm that supported her business with this type of help?
- What alternatives have been considered to resolve this issue? (Different solutions or other competitive organisations?)

Once the consultant has the answers to these questions (and any subsequent questions that arise due to the information provided by the client) he is then in the position to say 'OK, let me now give you a couple of options as to how we could help you get to where you want to go more quickly, with greater certainty and less pain.'

Key skills in ascertaining the client's requirements and confirming our understanding

- Preparing appropriate questions.
- Asking short, penetrating, open questions which encourage more detailed responses. ('When you address the issue, who will be involved?')
- Avoiding rambling questions that come in five parts or end up as multiple-choice options.
- Avoiding answering our own questions (e.g. 'How do you feel about that? I guess that must prove very expensive? I suppose this is something you will want to act on? I would certainly want to do something about it if I were in your shoes.').
- Giving the client time to answer.
- Listening to understand and putting aside any preconceptions so that we can hear what the client is telling us.
- Funnelling – building each subsequent question logically on the response received to the preceding question.
- Unbundling things that the client says which are not clear or are open to ambiguous interpretation. ('I'm interested in what you've just said – particularly

the bit about "even now". What did you mean by that?')

- Summarising our understanding of what we have been told. ('So the appraisal system is an issue for the business. However, you do not perceive it as critical because, first, your people are, in the main, finding a way of working around the problem, and second, there is no point in addressing the situation until the new divisional structure is up and running. Have I got that right?')

- Demonstrating that we are on the same wavelength. ('I sense that decision frustrates you.')

These ideas on how to sell additional or new services to existing clients build on, and are in addition to, the ideas we presented in Chapters 6 and 7 of *Creating New Clients*. In our previous book we addressed the subjects of positioning the firm with someone we had never previously met and understanding the situation and requirements of a non-client.

The E and S of the PACES process

In Chapters 8 and 9 of *Creating New Clients* we explored in depth how to take forward a selling opportunity once it has been uncovered. Whilst these ideas were presented in the context of a potential new-client scenario, the principles are totally transferable to the existing client situation. We could simply repeat these two chapters in this book but we feel this would provide little value to those people who have already invested in our previous publication. What is critical is that once we have identified an opportunity, we then manage the opportunity and through this management process bring home a greater percentage of wins.

OPPORTUNITY MANAGEMENT

More and more firms want to measure what is 'in the pipeline'. Understandably they want to have some measure of how the time and money put into marketing and selling is shaping up in terms of potential future business. It is not uncommon today for professionals to be asked to submit a forecast of potential future work.

These forecasts are usually badly flawed. Depending on the nature of the person submitting the forecast, they can be hopelessly over-optimistic or depressingly pessimistic. This is because there is no agreed process or structure for evaluating business in the pipeline. One person's 70 per cent probability is another's 10 per cent. Often the value of the opportunity is multiplied by a percentage that represents the likelihood of winning. A £100,000 opportunity at 50 per cent is calculated as having a weighted value of £50,000. We know of some professionals who reject the whole concept of percentage weighted opportunities. Their argument is that one either wins 100 per cent of the business or none.

Our opinion is that these percentages have little value – but not for the reason given above. We believe they have little value because they cause professionals to focus on the wrong things. Even if a 70 per cent evaluation is mathematically accurate, this is not the most important figure in any case. It is much more important to understand the 30 per cent of doubt that still exists.

It is rare that someone is able to convince us they know exactly where their doubts lie – that they know where the gaps in their knowledge exist or where exactly their competitive position needs strengthening. It is rarer still to see a Plan of Action in place to correct these shortcomings. What we mostly see is a piece of business forecast at 70 per cent and the professional waiting by the telephone to find out whether seven out of the ten opportunities so forecast turn into work.

Opportunity measurement and opportunity management are not the same things. We must understand the gap between where we are today with an opportunity and a 100 per cent certainty of winning. Once we know the constituent parts of this gap we can do something about filling it – turning the 70 per cent probability into an 80 per cent probability and the 80 per cent into 90 per cent.

The PACE opportunity management process

Our opportunity management process does not use percentages because we find these lead to a focus on the wrong number. Our process uses four levels – each level taking us a step closer to winning the opportunity we have found (Table 5.1).

The aim is to be able to answer the 'driving questions' that constitute each level. Once we can answer all the questions related to the first level, the opportunity is forecast as Q1. When we can answer all the 'driving questions' related to the second level, the opportunity is forecast as Q2 – and so on. One of the benefits of our process is that it can be tailored to any firm's opportunity management criteria.

As an example we have taken the HR Consultancy referred to in other parts of this chapter and constructed an opportunity management system for them.

Table 5.1: The PACE opportunity management process

Class	Qualification criteria	The driving questions
Qualified Opportunity Level 1 **Q1**	1. Opportunity identified 2. Discussions initiated 3. Our solution possible 4. Our type of client	Have we met with at least one person who has sufficient authority to give us a clear brief of requirements? Do we know that there is a problem or opportunity (agreed by the client) which needs resolution? Can we address the requirements? Is our solution likely to be technically acceptable? Is the prospect likely to be willing to pay for the added value areas that we typically incorporate in our solutions?

Table 5.1 (continued)

Class	Qualification criteria	The driving questions
Qualified Opportunity Level 2 **Q2**	1. Bases of decision understood 2. Business drivers understood 3. Budget situation understood 4. Players, timescales and Decision Making Process (DMP) understood 5. Pre-selling strategy and plan formulated	Do we fully understand their current and future situations? (e.g. structure, processes, systems) Do we fully understand the business imperatives driving this project? Do we know the opportunity costs of their current situation? As a corporate objective, how important is the project? Why? As a departmental objective, how important is this project? Why? Do we fully understand the positioning and synergy of other incumbent advisers? Do we understand the financial operations of this company? Do they have the money available? Which budget does this come from? Is the budget sufficient to cover our solution? Who is the budget-holder? Could more money be found? If so, from where? Do we know all of the players in the DMP? Who are they? Have we met them? Do we know what their roles will be? Do we know the **process** by which this decision will be reached? What is this? Do we know the requirements and Bases of Decision of all of the players involved? Have we identified the person who will make the final decision? Has the decision-maker committed to make a decision? Do we know their timescales for agreement and project execution?

Table 5.1 (continued)

Class	Qualification criteria	The driving questions
Qualified Opportunity Level 3 **Q3**	1. Short-listed, competitors known 2. Solution technically and financially acceptable 3. Talking with decision-maker and key influencers	Have we presented a solution which has been cost-justified? Has the client dedicated time/effort/resource/to fully evaluate our solution? How has this been carried out? Has the validity of our solution been accepted and agreed by all the key players involved in the decision? Have the key players told us that they particularly like aspects of our solution? What are these aspects? Do we know all of the other alternatives they are considering? Are there no more than two other competitors still in the race? Do we know the offerings being made by the competitors? Have we created a requirement for Unique Selling Points (USPs) which only we can provide? Have our competition created a requirement for USPs which we will find difficult/impossible to provide? Have we got alternatives/arguments to deflect the competitors' USPs? Have we presented these to the key players? Do we know, if our proposal is accepted, what the different individuals involved in the DMP, may have to sacrifice?

Table 5.1 (continued)

Class	Qualification criteria	The driving questions
Qualified Opportunity Level 4 **Q4**	1. Verbal commitment 2. 'Closing meeting' fixed 3. Paper trail understood	Have we met the bases of decision of all the key players? Are we in a 'short list of one' with the business only subject to discussion and negotiation on final details? Has the decision-maker (or her direct messenger) actually told us that we have won the business? Is a 'closing meeting' arranged? Do we understand, in detail, the client's paper trail – how, when, where and by whom the decision will be ratified from their side? Have we triggered the client's internal mechanism for raising the necessary documentation that will allow us to invoice for work and be paid accordingly? Have we developed any genuine allies during our selling process?

Opportunity management systems

This type of opportunity measurement can be provided on computer. This allows a summary report to be drawn up of all opportunities that a practice area or firm may have 'on the boil'. It shows where we are (Q1 to Q4) in respect of all of these opportunities.

We have clients who understand the reason for our reluctance to use percentages but who have chosen to ignore our opinions. Instead of a Q1 to Q4 rating they have substituted percentages at the different levels (e.g. Q1 = 20 per cent and Q4 = 90 per cent). They can then produce reports that show the total of the weighted values per professional, department or practice area.

Returning to our insistence on opportunity management – not opportunity measurement – the most important screen is the one which shows a summary of the actions that still need to be taken to advance our position with each opportunity.

Our HR consultant, having discovered the opportunity for helping his client establish divisional recruitment and induction practices and training people in these practices, may return to his office convinced he has an opportunity that can be classified as Q1. He can fully and confidently answer all of the driving questions related to this level. To raise the opportunity to level Q2, he has more work to do. The 'driving questions' spell out clearly what this work is.

In Chapter 8, 'Using Supporting Technology', we will return to this subject of computer-based support.

The HR consultant's plan of action

To progress his opportunity from Q1 into the realms of Q2, the plan of action could look as follows.

- At next meeting with HRD (date agreed) address the following:
  - Current providers of HR advice and their potential role in helping with this issue.
  - Relationship between current advisers and client organisation.
  - In-depth investigation of current processes – including supporting documentation.
  - Detailed understanding of all timescales related to execution of work and decision-making.
  - Continued clarification of the new budgeting process.
- Agree with HRD the principle of a meeting (minimum telephone discussion) with each of the new divisional heads to understand their perspective, their priorities and bases of decision.
- Find out from divisional heads whom they will involve in reaching a decision on how to find the right support regarding new HR practices, procedures and training.
- Formulate ongoing pre-selling plan on the basis of above.

SUMMARY

Selling more of our products, services and capabilities to our existing clients is the best way to increase fee income. The principles are straightforward.

- Train all client-facing people so that they have a deep understanding of clients' industries, clients' businesses and the issues which face these industries and businesses. Given this knowledge, most professionals will be able to recognise the first glimmering of an opportunity to help clients further – because they will understand the context and probable importance of the opportunity.
- When seeking new products to sell to clients, look firstly at the expertise that has already been developed as a result of demands arising from other clients' work. Seek to multiply the success of a proven solution rather than searching for a ground-breaking, brilliant solution that solves a problem no one has yet recognised.
- When pursuing an identified potential opportunity, follow the PACES process – and stick closely to the order of the process.
- Before seeking to discuss new areas of work with a client, position the firm's credibility and credentials in these fields.
- Put time and effort into understanding the client's situation and requirements.
- Train people in the skills of questioning and listening. These are degradable skills, not everlasting areas of knowledge.

- Sort the real opportunities from the 'phantoms' by explicitly asking the client about the impact and significance of the opportunity identified. Is the client searching for a solution and, if so, how critical is this to the client's organisation?
- Manage the selling process by 'knowing what we don't know' and knowing our comparative competitive weaknesses and strengths. Knowledge of these factors creates the basis of a plan of action that will increase our chances of winning the work.

FIRST STEPS

1. Select one of your Key Clients. Spend one hour per week for the next two months building up your knowledge of this client's marketplace by

   - asking colleagues who are considered expert in this market arena;
   - reading one or two trade journals;
   - searching the Internet;
   - attending relevant conferences.

   In month three ask people in your own organisation and in the client (if appropriate) what this client's objectives, strategies and plans are for the future. Also select a second Key Client on which to start the above process.

   In this way you will be positioned in the future to spot, and possibly develop, new opportunities for the firm within these clients.

2. Compare your selling skills to those demonstrated in Scenes 1 to 5 in this chapter. If you feel there are gaps in your skills, source some training or coaching in this area to help you to make the most of every opportunity (seen or unseen) in your Key Clients.

3. Apply the PACE opportunity management process to an opportunity you are currently pursuing. Answer all the driving questions honestly and put together an action plan designed to increase your chances of success.

Chapter 6 **Cross-selling to Clients**

EASY CONCEPT, DIFFICULT APPLICATION

A partner in a large multidisciplinary firm recently said to us, 'Ninety-two per cent of the work that we could potentially carry out for our clients goes to other advisers.' That sounded like a high number to us, but we were not going to argue over a few percentage points, and in any case our client had the information which supported his statement. The partner went on to voice the inevitable conclusion that if only his firm could cross-sell effectively, all their fee income objectives for the next five years would be blown out of the water. The one small consolation for this partner was that his firm's problem was shared by all of his competitors.

So why is it that this obvious and easy source of generating additional fee income should be so difficult to marshal – and what are the solutions?

We will examine four important issues. These are:

1. The image in the client's mind.
2. The silo syndrome.
3. Lack of knowledge of the firm's capabilities.
4. The wrong technique when cross-selling.

THE IMAGE IN THE CLIENT'S MIND

We examined this issue in Chapter 4. What we are as a firm is what each individual client believes us to be. Our positioning becomes fixed in the client's mind. If we have solely provided technical expertise on indirect taxation issues for the last ten years, it is hardly surprising that we fail to automatically come to mind when the opportunity for due diligence work arises.

In that chapter we addressed in some detail how to focus Capability Marketing activities in order to begin to break down the paradigms that our clients may have of our firm.

THE SILO SYNDROME

This was a terminology used by one of our clients. This client was not referring to her firm: she was referring to her department! She stated simply, 'Too often our people work in silos.' The people who carried out compliance tax work did not talk with the people who carried out tax advisory work despite the fact that they were working for the same clients.

The people who obtained their work from the front office people (dealers and traders) within their merchant bank clients did not have any communication with those people who carried out the corporate tax advisory work for the people in the merchant banks' back offices.

The people dealing with the merchant bank front offices were a very capable crew, but the rest of the department regarded them as somewhat arrogant and definitely elitist. The poor folk who specialised in compliance work were seen by everyone as the lowest caste even though these people, who had regular opportunities to delve into all aspects of a client's tax affairs, were the best placed to find new opportunities for advisory work. It goes without saying that cross-selling was poor. Compliance specialists were even accused of carrying out some advisory work to boost their utilisation and spice up their dreary lives!

Having the different departments on different floors hardly helped matters.

Client and team orientation

For decades most professional services firms were organised along practice group lines. There would be a Litigation Department, an Employment Law Division, a Property Services Section and so on. This is beginning to break down, more quickly in some firms than others. The main advantage of such a structure is that it makes the business easy to manage. A partner who has spent his life in audit runs an audit department. He can uphold quality standards, he can ensure that his people receive the right technical training, he knows the expected utilisation and recovery levels for audit work, and he can therefore police these. The traditional organisational structure has everything to do with firm governance and nothing to do with the client. This structure is also the classic fertile ground for silo thinking.

Recognising that clients wanted more than plain vanilla advice, that they wanted advice specific to their organisation in their business sector, the 1990s in particular saw professional services firms begin to organise their businesses along market sector lines in an attempt to become more market facing. A chosen market sector could be property and construction. A department would be formed to focus on clients and prospective clients in this market arena. The department would include professionals from the firm's various practice areas. In reality this often meant that the project management specialists would seek their work in this sector independently of the quantity surveyors who worked totally in isolation from the environmental consultants. Occasionally a major business opportunity, in which the client demanded a number of disciplines, forced the practice areas to work together.

To become a truly client-facing organisation – and to have any hope of creating the right environment for cross-selling – this process has to go further. Professional services firms must, particularly in relation to their Key Clients and Crown Jewels, organise themselves in multidisciplinary client-orientated teams.

In the main, when it comes to cross-selling, professionals do not recommend other parts of their firm: they recommend other professionals within their firm in whom they have trust and confidence. When working on a project with a client, a human resources consultant may come across a systems issue which needs the intervention of an IT consultant. The HR specialist's position may be that he

- knows nobody in his firm's IT practice;
- met a couple of IT 'bods' at the firm's annual do. They were well under the influence and were especially rowdy – so he was not at all impressed;
- has heard that the IT practice is a bit thin;
- has been told by others that Hunt & Shoesmith's IT people are really the best in the business.

Given this scenario, he is unlikely to recommend that his client speak with the IT specialists within his firm; in fact he is likely to keep very quiet. If the IT boys come in to fix the HR system and they foul up (which seems to the HR consultant to be a distinct possibility) his work is likely to be delayed, at best. At worst, it may be cancelled. His client could even blame him personally for recommending these cowboys and the entire relationship could be put at risk. No, best say nothing.

But does the image in the HR consultant's mind bear any resemblance to reality? He has a picture picked up from snippets of experience and snatches of hearsay. The real evidence is thin but his image of the IT practice is off-putting enough for the cross-selling opportunity to pass him by.

This is a major issue in accountancy firms. Traditionally most clients have been 'owned' by the audit practice. Today such firms realise that their fee growth ambitions can only be met by selling other services to their client base. Despite this we still hear of audit partners keeping their colleagues from other disciplines at arm's length from their clients by claiming that 'the time is not right' and 'they (their clients) have other priorities right now'.

On numerous occasions we have been told by specialist areas of such firms that they find it easier to develop business from totally new clients than to fight the audit partner who seems intent on blocking their every approach to 'his client'.

From the other (audit) side of the fence we have heard the words, 'They won't even turn up unless they think the project is worth more than £250,000 and when they do get a big piece of work their attitude is rape, burn, pillage and then walk away.' (Audit partner speaking about the firm's IT practice.) Unfortunately, these represent typical examples of silo behaviour exacerbated by silo organisational structures.

The simple answer is that people must either be encouraged or (if necessary) forced to work together. Whilst all parts of the same organisation have the option to stand at a distance from each other and whilst their objectives are mutually exclusive, they will at best not work together cohesively and at worst they will actually work against each other. Either way, cross-selling is a non-starter.

In Chapter 9 we will look in detail at how we organise a client-focused team to work together.

Fine words but contrary reality

It seems rather fashionable for groups of senior people in firms to go away together for a few days to agree the corporate vision. Hundreds of sheets of flip-chart paper and thousands of man-hours are used in capturing the essence of the firm's envisioned future, its core purpose and its core values.

James C. Collins and Jerry I. Porras, the two individuals considered to be the world's leading authorities on this subject (and authors of the bestseller *Built to Last*, Century Business Books, 1998) are categorical in their assertion that core values have to be discovered – they are not created. In other words a firm's core values are what the firm really is, what its 50 years of existence have made it, not what a group of senior partners would like to believe it should be. It is hardly surprising that after a senior partners' awayday when the glowing positive adjectives which are said to represent the firm's core values are later revealed to junior staff, they react with cynicism.

A firm we work with went away on such an event. In fairness to a number of the very senior people in this firm, they knew that the culture and values of the firm needed improvement. They wanted to change this and the exercise they carried out with a very large group of professional staff was to get them to agree what the desired culture and values *should* be. To co-ordinate all the thinking of this very large group was a massive undertaking, but the words and phrases which were agreed were very positive and uplifting. 'Committed to the development of our people', 'honesty in all our dealings', 'to value and demonstrate real teamwork'. All good stuff.

However, the real test follows. Will this firm uphold these values? Will there be reward and recognition for those who demonstrate these values and, as David Maister asks in Chapter 6 of his book *True Professionalism* (Free Press, 1997), what will be the sanction for non-compliance?

To create the right environment for cross-selling, we have to have people who are prepared to share and delegate. People must be targeted on the number of qualified introductions they provide to other practice disciplines. They must be recognised for this, paid a bonus for this, and receive partnership points for it. What sanction has ever been taken against a senior partner who hoarded all the work in a client for himself and his department? What does the good delegator get from the firm that the poor delegator does not?

Real teamworking is a major facilitator of regular cross-selling. So why is it that we have firms who talk teamwork but have no team objectives, and some of the few which do have team objectives have these in addition to (but in a definite second place to) individual objectives? Why is it that firms talk of collective ownership but reward on personal performance?

There are some fundamental structural, cultural, organisational, motivational and behavioural issues which need to be addressed if a firm is to have any hope of unleashing the full potential of its cross-selling opportunities. Firms have to walk the talk.

LACK OF KNOWLEDGE OF THE FIRM'S CAPABILITIES

When running a training course where the participants may not know each other, it is common practice within the first few minutes of such an event to have people introduce themselves to their colleagues. With a number of our larger professional services clients one individual's introduction can often be followed by someone else remarking, 'I didn't know we did that!'

This is not a problem associated only with large firms: it is also commonly found in small practices. In the authors' own firm we do not find it easy to constantly keep up to date on all the new concepts and programmes just seven or eight colleagues are developing.

In all professional firms cross-selling opportunities are missed simply because the professional on the spot recognises a potential issue but does not associate the issue with his firm's capabilities or services. At best we hear people say things such as, 'That may be something we could help you with. I'm not exactly sure. What I will do is ask around in the most likely places when I get back to the office. If there is something we can do I'll give you a call.' For a client facing a problem or opportunity she wishes to resolve with certainty, this is not positive, reassuring language.

If a firm wishes to cross-sell its services effectively, it has to ensure that its people have sufficient current knowledge of the firm's products, services, capabilities and people resources to be able to immediately advise the client as to whether it has the capability to assist. Impossible in a fast-growing and ever-changing firm? Not today. In Chapter 8 we explain how all client-facing people can have instant access to all the firm's potential solutions.

THE WRONG TECHNIQUE WHEN CROSS-SELLING

Given that we can in some way overcome the teamworking difficulties we have outlined above, there is still another hurdle to overcome. So often well-intentioned attempts to cross-sell fail because they are executed incorrectly. Perhaps the best way to illustrate this is to give two examples. Scenario 1 will provide a typical example of what we hear when we ask professionals to recount a cross-selling attempt which seemed to fall on stony ground.

Scenario 1

Partner: I understand that one of the initiatives on the horizon is to appoint a consultancy to help you create an electronic sales management system for your organisation?

Client: *That's right. We've realised that we cannot continue with the mounds of paper and the home-brewed computer system we're using now. We need one co-ordinated system we can use right across the organisation. We're some way down the line with our thinking and we're going to begin to talk with some consultants over the next few weeks.*

Partner: Something you're probably not aware of is that we have a sister division which specialises in this area – Salesforce Automation, systems and so on. I think it would be opportune for you to speak with them. I'd like to introduce you to a colleague of mine, John Gleeson, who specialises in this area. I think he would be worth meeting.

Client: *R . . . r . . . right. Without being rude, time now is of the essence and what we're trying to do is to get this thing under way as soon as possible. We've been very selective about the people we have asked to speak with and we believe we've picked a number of organisations whom we feel will add value to this process. Again, not wanting to be rude, what can your colleague do which the other people we're talking with, cannot?*

Partner: Well, John is recognised as a true expert in this arena. He was one of the original people who designed sales-force systems. He worked in sales management himself for a number of years and has a practitioner's approach to systems creation. I'm sure you would find it a good investment of your time talking with him.

Client: *Tell you what, get John to drop me a line giving me some details abut the sort of work he has done and the kind of things he could bring to a situation like ours. Perhaps he can also send me a brochure. If it looks like he can add something to what we're considering already, we can consider talking with him.*

This is a polite brush-off. In not so many words the client has said she is not convinced and has said 'No' to meeting the new professional.

Scenario 2

Partner: I understand that one of the initiatives on the horizon is to appoint a consultancy to help you create an electronic sales management system for your organisation?

Client: *That's right. We've realised that we cannot continue with the mounds of paper and the home-brewed computer system we're using now. We need one co-ordinated system we can use right across the organisation. We're some way down the line with our thinking and we're going to begin to talk with some consultants over the next few weeks.*

Partner: Something you're probably not aware of is that we have a sister division which specialises in this area – Salesforce Automation, systems and so on. I think it would be opportune for you to speak with them. I'd like to introduce you to a colleague of mine, John Gleeson, who specialises in this area. I think he would be worth meeting.

Client: *R . . . r . . .right. Without being rude, time now is of the essence and what we're trying to do is to get this thing under way as soon as possible. We've been very selective about the people we have asked to speak with and we believe we've picked a number of organisations whom we feel will add value to this process.*

Again, not wanting to be rude, what can your colleague do which the other people we're talking with, cannot?

Partner: John *is* an expert in this field but that's not the main benefit as I see it. The benefit in talking with John is not just in what John brings – but in what John's business and ours together can bring. One of the key processes that any consultancy will have to go through in order to put together a system which fits your business is to map the sales process. As you know, in your organisation this is both varied and complex.

If you think back to the research we did to construct your training programme and also the close association we have had with your Business Development Team over the last two years, we already have this informally documented. Working with John it would take very little to convert this into a formal map of your sales processes.

We can make this knowledge available to John. This costs you nothing and is almost certain to make your overall investment less. Not only that, it could save an enormous amount of time and cause less disruption. There are a number of other areas in which we could also co-operate and make your life easier, make the finished product more robust and save you money in the process. I believe it is worth your while talking with John.

Client: *It sounds like it will be worthwhile including him. Get him to call my secretary or me and fix up a meeting.*

Partner: I'll do that and I'll also spend time with him over the next few days giving him a thorough briefing on your organisation. Would it be helpful if I invested some time to attend this first meeting as well? Whilst you and he will be the main players I may be able to make some contribution from the experiences we've gained through working with you in the past.

Client: *Sounds a good idea. I'll be pleased to meet with you both.*

We have found that when professionals are convinced of the value of cross-selling they are convinced on the basis of its value to their firm. However, this is of no consequence to the client and it is certainly of no benefit to the client.

In the first scenario the recommendation to meet with John Gleeson does nothing for the client other than potentially eat up more of her valuable time. In the second scenario the professional has thought in advance about the benefits to the client of meeting this other person from his firm. He positions these benefits well and the client is persuaded to at least include the John Gleeson character in her first round of discussions on the subject of the new systems requirement.

FIRST STEPS

1. Take time once a month to visit one of your counterparts in another part of the firm. Give him an opportunity to give you information on the services his team provides that might be needed by your clients. Then take the time to explain your services to him.

    Over the following months keep in touch with the people you meet that you would be comfortable introducing to your clients at the right time. If possible, actually arrange client meetings to their benefit.

    In a year's time you will have built a network of contacts whose services you can introduce to clients and who can cross-sell for you.

2. If you have responsibility for a team of professionals, ensure that team members are recognised and rewarded for the contribution they make to the team and not just to their individual objectives. Make this recognition very visible to the whole team.

3. When you identify a cross-selling opportunity, think through, and sell, the **extra** value your client will gain from buying this expertise from your firm **because** of the work you already carry out for them.

Section 3 **Key Client Planning**

Chapter 7 **Forming the Plan**

One thing we have learned over the years is never to answer the question, 'So what should a Key Client plan look like?' We have found that the best answer to this question is another question: 'What do you think you will be able to implement and manage on an ongoing basis?' In other words, 'What plan will work for you?'

In our work we have come across dozens of examples where attempts at Key Client management have been made but have ended in failure. The early part of these scenarios is familiar. Someone believes that the firm could manage its client base better and that this would lead to more work being won. The next step varies. Sometimes this person produces a form of Key Client plan which is then introduced to the rest of the firm or practice area. Sometimes the firm recruits an outside 'expert' who has experience of working with Key Client management (nearly always in a non-associated industry). Sometimes a committee is formed to formulate the ideal Key Client plan. The final option is to use consultants who have experience of this type of work.

The vast majority of these attempts are stillborn, and the few that are implemented rarely have any impact after the first few months: they are a passing fad. The main reasons for this are:

- The format of the plan usually grows like Topsy as various people have their input into it. The resultant plan that has to be implemented across the firm's Key Clients is seen to be difficult, time-consuming and unwieldy.
- The format of the plan seems custom-designed for the most complex client the firm possesses. In most other client situations the plan is over-engineered.

When we meet these failed attempts at Key Client planning and ask to see the format of the plans the firm was attempting to implement, we invariably see more good than bad. The problem is that the firm has worked under two misapprehensions. These are:

1. The more comprehensive the plan, the better.
2. There has to be one format for all Key Client plans across the firm (or practice area).

As we have already indicated, comprehensiveness may be the death of the Key Client plan. Also, who said that there should be one format for Key Client planning per firm? Is every Key Client the same? Do they have the same value to our firm? Are they all under the same level of threat from our competitors? Do they all have the same potential? Why can't we have four different Key Client plan formats – or five, come to that? Why not tailor the format of the plan to the type of Key Client that we are addressing?

We learned long ago never to try to provide a definitive answer to the question about what a Key Client plan should look like, because we run the risk of driving our client down the road of an unsuccessful implementation.

In this chapter we will examine the various options and formats for a Key Client plan – from the most simple to the most comprehensive. We do not believe that simpler is better or that bigger is better. We believe that the format of the ideal plan will

- fit the Key Client around whom we have built the plan;
- be manageable and sustainable.

THE BASIC ELEMENTS OF A KEY CLIENT PLAN

The simplest Key Client plan contains two elements – *Objectives* and a *Plan of Action*. Except for some basic information on the client – name of the organisation, address, telephone, name of our contacts, e-mail addresses (the sort of things that would appear on an old-fashioned box file card) – there is nothing else. In paper format this plan takes one or two sheets.

Objectives

Whether we are formulating the most simple Key Client plan or the most comprehensive, objectives should meet certain criteria. Objectives should be SMART. The acronym SMART has been around for years and different authors would have it mean different things. Our version of SMART is as follows. Objectives should be:

Specific.
Measurable.
Achievable.
Responsibility allocated.
Timebound.

Specific
'We will build closer ties with Client A' is very woolly and non-specific. 'We will increase our RPI index from 18 to 27 through achieving regular contact with the senior Human Resources team in Client A' is an example of a specific objective.

Measurable
The previous example of a specific objective is also measurable. If we are successful we will be able to measure an improvement – from 18 to 27 in our RPI. (You will find more information on RPI later in this chapter under the heading 'Useful tools'.)

Achievable

Nothing is more likely to kill off ongoing enthusiasm for Key Client planning than unachievable objectives. Unrealistic targets result in unproductive client review meetings. Were the objectives unrealistic or was the execution at fault? Fruitless debate ensues. Whenever there is a strong case for the former, it puts the whole process of Key Client planning in question and reduces professionals' motivation to be involved. After all, who wants to be involved in 'failures'? There is no mileage in pipe dreams.

Responsibility allocated

We accept total responsibility for the clumsiness of this expression but we have not found a version of SMART that contains specific reference to where the buck stops.

In our experience the implementation of Key Client plans in professional firms usually involves more than one person from the firm. Very often the execution of these plans can involve many people. Too many times we see plans formulated where it is unclear who has the ultimate responsibility for an objective to be met or an action to be carried through. We support the whole notion of teamworking in a Key Client environment. However, teamworking must not be a synonym for collective lack of accountability.

Timebound

By when should this objective be achieved? If actions have to be put in place, when should these begin? Is there a critical path of actions that needs to occur? If so, in what order should they happen?

Types of Objectives

Objectives can be set on numerous criteria. Here are some examples:

- *Increased fee income.* 'To increase fee income from £35,000 to £50, 000 over the next twelve months.'
- *Increased profitability.* 'To introduce and train currently under-utilised consultants to carry out at least 80 per cent of the compliance-level work within this client during the next two quarters.'
- *New fee income.* 'To win at least one corporate finance-related engagement by the end of the fiscal year.'
- *New relationships.* 'To build contacts with technical division senior staff with a view to being seen as a credible speaking partner.' (Measurements – invitations to 'talk ideas', discussion papers requested, inclusion on tender lists.)
- *Strengthened relationships.* 'To ensure that the senior partner engages in face-to-face, meaningful, business-related dialogue with the FD and/or MD on a minimum of three occasions during the next year.'

Plans of Action

If an objective is *what* we plan to achieve with a Key Client over a period of time, the plan of action is *how* we will go about the tasks which will give us the greatest chance of achieving the stated objective.

Plans of Action should be SMART in the same way as Objectives – and for exactly the same reasons.

- Do we have a clear idea of the actions that need to happen? (Specific.)
- Will we definitely know when these actions have occurred? (Measurable.)
- Are these planned actions realistic? (Achievable.)
- Who is responsible for making these actions happen? (Responsibility allocated.)
- When will these actions begin? In what order will they happen? When should we have carried out these actions? (Timebound.)

Project management and Key Client management

Sometimes professionals hold back from embracing the discipline of Key Client planning and Key Client management as it is perceived as yet another thing to learn – another skill to develop on top of all the others. For many professionals we would suggest that they not look at the differences in this 'new' discipline, but look at the similarities with other processes carried out today.

In some areas of professional services engagements where the execution of work is complex, protracted and ever-changing, it has long been recognised that professionals need to treat the engagement as a true project. This involves the use of project management methodologies and project management tools such as Gantt charting. For professionals who already employ these processes, we would urge them to think about Key Client planning and the execution of Key Client plans as an extension of this discipline in which they already engage.

The tools are readily interchangeable. One of the benefits of a Gantt chart, for instance, is that it makes the Plan of Action readily visible: it turns words into a picture. Seeing the plan in graphic format very often highlights weaknesses in the links between various elements. It can highlight where unmanageable peaks of activity occur simultaneously. The plan can then be adjusted accordingly.

Whilst we do not wish to recommend any particular level of complexity for a Key Client plan, a Plan of Action which can be expressed in a visual format is usually helpful.

So what could the simplest 'non-visual' Key Client plan look like? We provide an illustration in Table 7.1.

Table 7.1: A simple Key Client plan

SMART objectives	Ownership	Start Date	Completion
To be recognised as a genuinely supportive adviser through providing specific and valuable advice and help which will enable the client to successfully manage its Transition Programme over the next eighteen months. (Measurement in provision of written/verbal references.)	AM	Week 1	Week 52
To achieve at least £40,000 in additional fees through providing support for the Transition Programme.	AM	Week 1	Week 40

SMART plans of action	Ownership	Start Date	Completion
Meeting with JY and TR to more fully explore Operations involvement and concerns.	HW		Week 3
Meet with client's training providers with view to finding areas of mutual benefit and forming alliance.	JS		Week 4
Arrange meeting with FD and MD.	AM	Week 4	Week 5
Meeting with FD and MD re strategic issues and their view of gaps to be filled.	AM	Week 7	Week 9
Invite JY and TR to Walton – overview our technical capabilities. Stay overnight? Organise social meeting/meal with potential team members.	HW	After FD/MD meeting	No more than two weeks after
JY and TR at Walton.	HW		By week 13 at the latest
Present (in person) ideas paper to FD and MD – demonstrating value. All ideas must not have price tags attached!	AM		By week 14 at the latest
Set up round table meeting – JY, TR, FD and MD. AM, HW and two Ops specialists to attend.	AM		Within two weeks of ideas meeting

The two objectives are mutually supportive. The over-riding aim is to deliver value to the client which will result in a strengthening of the perceived position of the advisers. Achievement will be measured by the willingness of the client to provide unequivocal references regarding the value of the support provided. Whilst the Transition Programme extends for eighteen months, the aim is to be seen as an especially supportive adviser within the next twelve months.

However, the firm also sees this as a fee-earning opportunity and has set a minimum value on what it hopes to achieve from providing professional support to its client.

Even though our Objectives extend over a year, this Plan of Action only extends over sixteen weeks. This is the longest realistic time we believe we can plan actions ahead given this particular situation. The Plan of Action (and possibly the Objectives) will have to be reviewed.

The Plan of Action gets less certain (dates-wise) as time goes by; this is to be expected. One action depends upon the execution of previous actions. If this Plan of Action goes broadly as expected, there will be need for a plan review somewhere around Week 12.

How much goes into the Plan of Action is a matter of choice. When the second action is completed (JS to meet with client's training providers) we will probably expect some form of feedback from JS. This could be a written report, a summary of recommendations or verbal input at a Key Client planning meeting. Whether we choose to record this feedback mechanism as part of the Plan of Action is up to us. If we know that JS is a bit lax on marshalling his thoughts, we may include this action as part of our agreed plan.

Beyond the simple plan format

Every Key Client plan will have Objectives and Plans of Action. That is the common thread. However, the simplest plans will contain these two elements and nothing more. The question could (in fact, must) be asked, 'Why do we need anything more?'

The answers to this question lie in the origins of the Key Client Objectives and the strategies that lie behind the intended actions. In the simplest Key Client plans the origin of the objectives is 'top of the head' and the actions are 'logical ways forward'.

The resultant Objectives and Plans of Action may be the best and most appropriate for the client concerned. However, if we want to be more certain of this, we must consider the use of Key Client planning tools and examine the value of what we know (and don't know) about the client in question.

This is not meant to be a subtly implied criticism of the simplest Key Client plans. There are many occasions when this type of 'top of the head' plan is perfectly appropriate and fitting. A 'top of the head' plan is certainly better than no plan at all. To return to our earlier argument – why is it not OK to have four or five different types of Key Client plans to reflect the complexity of the client and the value of the client to our firm? One format could be the simple Objectives/Plan of Action variety.

We will now move forward to examine the tools we can also use to help us formulate our Objectives and Plans of Action and the types of information that can potentially help us to out-think our competitors. How many of these tools we choose to use and how much of this information is considered vital background to a Key Client plan is a matter of personal preference.

USEFUL KEY CLIENT PLANNING TOOLS

Relationship Protection Index (RPI)

Imagine that a firm is examining the relationship it has with two of its clients – we will call them Client A and Client B. The value of both of these relationships seems very similar when measured by both fee income and profitability. The firm wants to form a view as to which of these two clients is the most likely source of ongoing fee income.

There is an argument that says this is the most valuable measure of a client. Past income has been received and spent. The value of this has gone. The value of a client is only in what they will provide in the future. We do not want to become involved in an academic debate on this issue, but the point certainly has some value.

The Client A situation

Our relationship with Client A is simple and straightforward. Our partner responsible for this relationship handles everything. He meets with his opposite number within the client (the Financial Director) twice a year. Meetings are formal and well structured.

If there are any client requirements falling out of these meetings, the partner concerned will manage the selling and proposal creation and delivery process. Unfortunately we have never found an opportunity for work over and above the partner's specialism – which is audit and accountancy.

The Client B situation

In Client B we do not earn the same volume of audit and accountancy fees, but the overall fee income is equal to that of Client A. The partner responsible for Client B has been proactive in introducing capable people into the relationship with the client. In particular he has a senior manager who can act as his stand-in – and does so when he is either on holiday or involved in time-consuming client work elsewhere.

Not only has he introduced a senior manager from his own discipline, he has also been instrumental in introducing another partner from his firm's taxation practice as well as people from his firm's Strategic Consultancy arm. This has resulted in his firm winning more and more of the client's specialist taxation work and there is hope that the compliance work will now follow. The strategy consultants carried out a project two years ago and are now seen as regular speaking partners by the client. However, we have to bear in mind that the client produces much smaller audit fees, and the total of all the fees earned from this client only matches the audit fees of Client A.

With Client B we have service review meetings. These occur twice a year. The audit partner, the taxation partner and the head of the Strategic Consultancy team all attend. They meet with a client team of between five and seven. The financial director is always present and on most occasions so is the managing director.

In addition to this type of meeting, in the Client B scenario every attempt is made to involve each of the client's board members in at least one of the firm's 'events' each year. Different things appeal to different board members. Some enjoy certain types of entertainment and will give up either business time or their personal time to participate in this. A couple of the board see this as 'frivolous' so the partner responsible for Client B makes every effort to personally invite them to appropriate seminars and conferences where he feels they may find value in investing their time.

However, we have to return to the bottom line. The relationship with Client B is no more profitable than the relationship with Client A. The question here, however, is not about past fee income or past profitability. The question, if we were taking a bet, is: *Which one of these relationships would we bet on continuing to produce profitable fee income in three years' time?*

Instinctively and intuitively we know the answer. The relationship with Client B is well developed. The relationship with Client A is at risk. It is a 'point-to-point' relationship. If the partner responsible for Client A wins the Lottery and retires, our entire relationship is at risk. If the financial director leaves his post (or is asked to leave!) it appears that we have no other senior contacts. If our competitors take one piece of work from us we lose the entire client and the whole relationship because there is only one piece of work we carry out!

The Relationship Protection Index (RPI) replaces the instinct and intuition we used to decide on the differences in quality of the Client A/Client B relationships with a simple model. In real life the differences in the quality of client relationships are rarely so starkly contrasted as in our opening example. Sometimes we intuitively feel we have an excellent relationship with a particular client, but examination using the RPI can highlight room for considerable strengthening.

Constructing and using an RPI

There are four stages involved in constructing and using a Relationship Protection Index. They are as follows:

1. Select the factors which we believe are indicative of the quality of relationships we seek to have with our Key Clients and put into place some form of 'scoring system'.
2. Take each of our Key Clients and Crown Jewels Clients in turn and measure them against the benchmarks we have set for the relationship criteria.
3. On the assumption there is a shortfall between the score a Key Client has achieved and the maximum possible, set an objective for a higher score to be achieved at some point in the future (possibly three to six months).
4. Formulate a Plan of Action that will see the RPI score increased to the desired level.

Stages 3 and 4 fit neatly into to the simple Key Client plan we looked at earlier in this chapter. What the RPI does is to inform our thinking and generate insights which help us to determine the relationship-building objectives we should be putting in place.

An RPI measurement could be formatted like the example in Table 7.2.

Table 7.2: Relationship Protection Index (RPI) measurement – an example

RPI factor	Score		
	0	**2**	**5**
Number of relationships with client's board members	One	Two or three	Four or more
Number of our people involved in client management	One	Two to four	Five or more
Number of our services utilised by client	One	Two	Three or more
Regularity of service review meetings with client	Not in place	In place but seen as limited value by client	In place and seen by client as valuable dialogue opportunity
Attendance at our 'events'	Rare or never	Occasionally	Regular attendees
Client a source of referrals	No	Infrequently	Regular – and also a reference point
Recognised 'added value' provided to client	None identified by client	Some small – moderate example(s)	Significant value recognised by client

How many factors for an effective RPI?

In theory we can have as few or as many factors as we like in our Relationship Protection Index. In reality the RPI works best with between six and twelve factors measured. Fewer than six and we will probably not form a rounded enough view of the relationship. More than twelve may lead us into 'analysis paralysis'.

How does the scoring work?

In Table 7.2 we have measured the RPI factors on a scale of 0, 2 and 5. There is nothing magical about these numbers: they are a personal choice. We have also decided that there should be three levels of measurement. There is no reason why this should not be four or perhaps even five. Again, we must simply avoid making the process too simplistic (two levels of measurement) or too complex (six or seven).

The choice of zero as the starting point is somewhat more than personal preference: there is a reason. The left-hand column represents the default position, i.e. to be doing work with a client someone in our firm has to be talking to someone in the client's organisation and by definition we will be providing them with at least one form of service or expertise. For that we score nothing. We only start to score when we improve on the default relationship. The only debate after that is the numbering which records the level of relationship achieved against any factor.

In our example we have chosen to use one form of scoring (0, 2 and 5) throughout the RPI. There is no reason why this has to be so. We have seen plenty of real-life examples where firms have weighted different factors due to their perceived relative importance.

Definitions

To get an accurate read on the quality of one relationship compared to another, we must compare like with like. It is important that when a firm or practice group sets up its RPI factors, it agrees the definitions in detail. The risk of not doing so is that we may believe we have a robust relationship with a particular client, only to be surprised by a competitor who finds it easy to take business that should have been ours. To illustrate our point on definitions we will examine some of the factors used in our example.

Number of relationships with client's board members

We need to agree the definition of a 'relationship'. Saying 'Hello' in the corridor when on the client's premises six weeks ago would not qualify.

Similarly, sharing a table at an industry function three years ago would also be a non-starter for claiming a 'relationship' with one of the client's board. If this factor is chosen (and it is a common and popular choice) it shows up the need to continually renew contacts with senior people within the client's organisation.

Number of our people involved in client management

We could have worded this differently. We could have called this factor 'number of people actively involved with client'. We chose not to as this could potentially include many professionals who are carrying out technical work. Some of these people could be operating in the background and the client may be totally unaware of them.

In our definition we mean those people who play an active part in the client service review meetings and who are involved in selling and managing work and projects. Again we would suggest that a time limit be set for qualification. If an active member of the client management team becomes disengaged for (say) nine months, then our potential score against this criterion reduces accordingly.

Number of our services utilised by client

This measurement should also have defined time limits. The definition may be more accurately defined as 'number of our services utilised by client in the last eighteen months'.

Regularity of service review meetings

In the right-hand column maximum points are scored if the client sees these as a valuable dialogue opportunity. Perhaps we would wish to tighten this definition up somewhat. Maybe we can only claim the five points if the client has *explicitly* said she values these meetings and she has said this at some point since the last two service reviews.

Attendance at our 'events'

The definitions we use to decide what constitutes an event are arbitrary. An event could be a business event (a seminar or round table) or an entertainment event (golf day or day at the races). It could include both of these. The only time we become pedantic over the definition is when professionals try to include lunch as an event. Giving up a day or half a day of one's personal or business time and choosing to be with one's advisers is a world away from agreeing to lunch. When the client agrees to lunch she is simply choosing to eat in a different venue. The sacrifice is small.

Client a source of referrals

If a client is really happy with the work we carry out for her, then she will often be willing to act as a reference point for other clients for whom we are seeking to carry out similar work. She may also be willing to proactively refer us to others within (and without) her firm whom she believes we may also be able to serve well.

Recognised 'added value' provided to client

We would suggest that we do not provide added value by doing excellent work. That is the client's reasonable expectation and is par for the course. Added value is something that we provide for the client, which the client finds valuable and did not expect as part of the relationship. The question on this factor is: have we delivered this type of unexpected input that the client has *explicitly* recognised as providing significant value?

Non-actionable RPI factors

With all of the factors we have given in our illustration, it is possible to do something about them if they are in need of improvement. We can work to create more relationships within the client. We can widen the contact surface from our side. We can make more effort to find the sorts of events that will appeal to our client's people – and so on. We can set an objective on what we would like to improve and then formulate a Plan of Action to achieve the objective.

When we have worked with our clients, helping them to construct their own Relationship Protection Index, we have often come across the situation where the client has recognised factors which give an indication of the strength of the relationship but about which they are powerless to do anything. Some examples of this are given in Table 7.3.

Table 7.3: Non-actionable Relationship Protection Index (RPI) measurement – an example

RPI factor	Score		
	1	**2**	**3**
Length of relationship with client	Less than one year	One year to ten years	Ten years plus
Number of direct competitors also working with client	More than three	One to three	None
Likelihood of acquisition by other companies	Possible to probable	Not very likely	Highly unlikely
Independence	Decisions at the mercy of parent	Part of a larger organisation but mostly independent	Totally independent

Could these factors influence our view as to the level of comfort we have over our relationship with the client? Of course they could.

Our advice, however, is not to mix up actionable and non-actionable factors if RPI is to be used as a Key Client planning input tool. We can have them both – but we must not mix them up.

Actionable and non-actionable RPI factors

It is possible to 'bolt on' a set of non-actionable criteria to our actionable RPI factors and simply measure them separately. For instance, we could put together the two examples given so far in this chapter. If we were to measure the strength of our relationship with any one client we could produce a number with a numerator (a measure on the actionable RPI factors) and a denominator (a measure on the non-actionable factors).

For instance, we could examine our relationship with a client and find that we score 26/6. A snapshot analysis of this number indicates that we have got a fairly strong relationship (26 out of a possible 35) but that the relationship is inherently weakened by factors outside of our control. There is not much point in worrying unduly about what we cannot affect – but we may as well recognise the threats. If the client is of real value to us we should be seeking ways to increase the score of 26 closer to the possible maximum of 35.

We have worked with RPI for years and have introduced it and applied it to scores of clients (not only in the professional services arena). What never ceases to amaze us is the imbalance between the measurable strength of relationships and the real value of the client to the business concerned. OK, very often the top two or three relationships may have a strong RPI score, but when we start looking at clients numbers four, five and six, we regularly find major relationships largely unmanaged and unprotected.

It is also not at all unusual to discover minor clients who receive huge amounts of love and attention – far more than their potential or strategic value would suggest is appropriate.

A word of warning

When we introduce RPI to our clients it has great impact – a real 'blinding flash of the obvious'. It is so often greeted as a method of really measuring how strong client relationships are – taking away the intuitive gut feel and replacing it with a solid yardstick. This is not the purpose. Knowing the index figure is not the end: it is the *means* to an end.

The aim of using RPI is to produce a Plan of Action that will ensure that the current business with our client is better protected in six months' time than it is now. The Plan of Action should also enable us to be better positioned to win more of the client's work which we do not have today; that is the purpose of the Relationship Protection Index.

Examples of actions arising from the use of the RPI tool

- In next meeting with FD raise the issue of service review meetings with the aim of agreeing these on a rolling tertial basis.
- Re-contact RG – Technical Director (lapsed contact). Invite her to be guest speaker at June technical workshop.
- TF reported extremely satisfied with our work. Approach him in next meeting with view to agreement to reference. Also request referrals into other departments.

Relationship Analysis Model (RAM)

The Relationship Analysis Model (Figure 7.1) seeks to provide us with an objective view of the value of the relationships we have with people within client organisations.

The upper box of the model has two axes. The horizontal axis represents the level of influence and power our contacts have within their organisations and particularly in relation to decisions to use (or not use) our firm. The further to the right we place an individual, the more influential we believe her to be.

The vertical axis represents these people's view of us and our firm. Do they love us? – in which case they are near the top of the axis, Do they really dislike us? – bottom of the axis – or are they somewhat indifferent? If this is the case, they live in 'No Man's Land'.

We have deliberately created 'No Man's Land'. There are a number of models like ours and mostly they ask for decisions as to where someone within the client is

Figure 7.1:   The Relationship Analysis Model

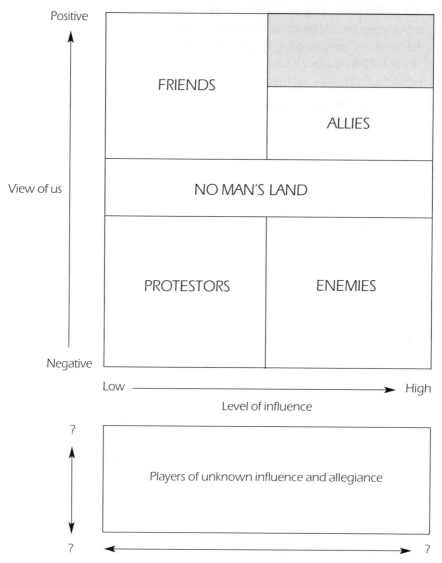

positioned. The choice is usually stark. Are they *for* us or are they *against* us? Our experience suggests that there are many people who are 'neutral'. They may also be neutral toward our competitors (with luck). There is no reason why these people should have negative feelings toward us – we have never delivered poor work or done anything to damage the relationship with them. Likewise we have probably done little or nothing to build a relationship with them – so why should we put on rose-tinted spectacles and say that because they don't hate us they must love us. They don't – they live in 'No Man's Land' – until we do something to move them from there.

The four other quadrants are:

- *Protestors.* These are people within our client who are not well disposed toward us but (at the moment) are unlikely to carry enough weight to negatively affect our incumbency.
- *Enemies.* Any people whom we perceive to be in this quadrant are real trouble. They are not only poorly disposed toward us, they have the muscle to do something about our position as an adviser to our client. The further to the bottom right-hand corner of the quadrant they are positioned, the greater the threat.
- *Friends.* Friends are people who like us but are not really in positions of influence. It is common that we mistake Friends for Allies – wanting to believe that those who are well disposed toward us are also in positions of influence.
- *Allies.* Our aim in any Key Client is to position the majority of our contacts in this quadrant. These people are supporters of our firm and they are in positions of power and influence. The upper shaded portion of this quadrant is the key area.

Players of unknown influence and allegiance

We have run a particular case study in some of our training workshops for years. The case study is built on the documented discussion between five senior directors of a business. These directors are in a board meeting, discussing the appointment of a PR agency.

After several pages of recorded discussion, the question is asked: 'Based upon all you have had the opportunity of hearing from the five directors, who will make the final decision regarding this project and who will be the key influencers?'

We break the training course participants into syndicates to pool their thoughts. On only one occasion in the last five years has any syndicate come up with the right answer. The correct answer is 'There is not enough information to be able to answer the question accurately.'

Why do we carry out this exercise? The exercise is a simulation of reality. It is common that when a professional finds an opportunity for new work within a client, someone asks the question 'Who will make the decision on this?' When did anyone receive the answer 'I don't know'? This answer is seen as a sign of failure. It is perceived as far better to name the obvious candidate within the client's organisation as the decision-maker than to admit to not knowing. However, any ensuing strategy is then founded upon a potentially erroneous assumption.

In fact the question 'Who will make the decision?' is not the right question to ask. The correct question is 'What will be the decision-making process with regard to this new opportunity?' This is a far bigger question. It asks for the stages the client will go through in coming to a conclusion. It asks who will be involved in the process. It asks for what their involvement will be. It asks about how much influence the people will have in respect of the decision, and it asks about who will give the final 'Yes' or 'No'.

We have also witnessed professionals using other well-known proprietary tools where part of the exercise is to position people within the client into certain parts of the model. Without fail, all of the known contacts are positioned somewhere – often upon the scantiest supporting information.

We have a 'No Man's Land' to position people within the client where we believe they are uncommitted neutrals. We have also built a 'catch all' box into which we drop all of those people within a client's organisation whom we feel may have some influence (but we are not sure how much) and about whom we know very little – or nothing – in relation to their perspective of our firm.

This model can be applied to a new business opportunity situation – to help us figure out the best-approach strategy. However, it also has a vital application in respect of how we plan to take forward an overall client relationship.

Using the model
Step 1
The first step in using the model is to position all of the players from the client's organisation. The key to this exercise is total honesty. We should be confident enough to say, 'I know I've been the client manager for this client for six years but I honestly don't know what influence the sales director has over our kind of assignments and I haven't a clue how he feels about us.' This is much better than 'I don't believe the sales director has much influence but he seems to like us' (based on the fact that he smiled during our last presentation to the board and did not ask any difficult questions).

In the first instance the sales director is positioned in the bottom box. In the second he is positioned as a Friend – and promptly forgotten about.

When analysing the relationships we possess within Key Clients, we may be carrying out this exercise as a team. It must be an accepted rule that anyone, right down to the most junior team member, can ask the question 'What evidence do you have for that conclusion?' That question, asked of the relationship with the sales director, would begin to show that the perception of him as a Friend was based on wishes and hopes and not on solid evidence.

On the assumption that our analysis has been honest and accurate, we should now have a visual summary of our key relationships within our client. The question is: what are we going to do with the information?

Step 2
The picture in front of us may suggest Objectives (e.g. 'We must develop a working relationship with the Birmingham-based R & D operation within the next year'). A 'working relationship' may be defined as regular face-to-face meetings with managers of the R & D division. On the other hand we may skip over the Objectives stage and simply put in place Plans of Action that 'leap off the page'.

We must continue our dialogue with Allies. We must seek ways to strengthen already good relationships. We must work on our Enemies. This is difficult; it may be unpleasant. It seems easier to keep at a distance from these individuals, but this stance will achieve very little. Enemies will simply be able to claim that their position is more justified as it is clear that the advisers are deliberately ignoring them.

We need to look carefully at the Protestors. This may seem the least fruitful area for action, but some Protestors will become the Enemies of the future as they rise in influence and power within their organisations. Ignoring or poorly treating junior people within a client is a sure way to create Protestors. Continuing to do the same to Protestors is a sure way to generate Enemies. What actions can we take to move Protestors closer to our Friends camp?

With regard to the unknown quantities that we have placed to the right in 'No Man's Land' and those people whom we have positioned as 'Players of unknown influence and allegiance', there are actions we clearly need to plan in order to get to know (and positively influence) these people.

It may appear that in a particularly large and complex client this model is going to suggest much relationship-building activity. Excellent – that is what is it meant to do. Where will we find this time? One source is the time we spend today with Friends. This can be a comfort zone for professionals – working with, talking to and entertaining those people we easily get on with and who are non-threatening. It is human nature after all – but not necessarily good Key Client management in a competitive marketplace.

SWOT Analysis

Probably the most common tool currently used in Key Client planning is the SWOT Analysis. Again, the value of a SWOT Analysis is not in the analysis itself – it is in what the analysis leads us to. The aim of the analysis is to give us insight into the relevant Objectives we should be setting ourselves in relation to a Key Client and the Plans of Action which will strengthen our relationship and see us win more fee-earning work in the future.

It is not unusual to discover confusion in the application of this simple tool. Typical of this are items that appear in the 'Weaknesses' category and then also appear as 'Threats'. A simple rule-of-thumb can be used here.

*   *Strengths and weaknesses* refer to factors over which we have, or should have, influence or control.
*   *Opportunities and threats* are factors over which we have no control. Our client, our client's marketplace, our client's competitors, our competitors, or even legislation and new regulations may trigger them.

The SWOT Analysis (if it is used as a Key Client planning tool) should be applied in relation to the particular client we are considering. It is not used in this instance as a general analysis of our firm's strengths, weaknesses, opportunities and threats. Also, what is important when we are working our way through a SWOT Analysis, is to take the client's view – particularly of our strengths and weaknesses. Reality (in this case) is in the perception of the client.

Figure 7.2:   SWOT Analysis: an example

S	W
Success in all previous implementation projects carried out for client.	Perception as an implenetation practice only.
Always invited to tender for all implementation projects – 'preferred supplier' status.	No international capability.
	No presence within US parent organisation.
Proven quantity of resource to man up to three major projects concurrently.	Contacts with senior strategy-makers in UK sporadic.
Strong project management skills.	Our Business Process Re-engineering arm not known within client.
Proven liaison capability between different concurrent projects.	
O	**T**
Demand from US parent to reduce costs will almost certainly result in radical new practices being required and new systems to support.	US parent may insist on international compatibility in future major IT projects.
	TSF (our competitor) regarded as logical 'systems strategy speaking partner'.
Meeting new Euro legislation on emissions will hasten search for new manufacturing processes – and supporting technology.	TSF have US presence and parentage.
	TSF acquisition of CDR in UK gives potential implementation capability.

One benefit of using a SWOT Analysis is that it organises our thinking. Sometimes people will claim 'We knew all that before'. There may be some truth to this, but usually the knowledge existed in a fragmented and disparate way. The SWOT Analysis brings this knowledge into an organised and visual structure. It also acts as a structured basis for discussion between the members of the team working with the Key Client.

Out of this analysis we may begin to see some goals emerging. For instance, in relation to the SWOT example above, the conclusions could be:

We need to build stronger relationships with the more senior people in the UK. We are coming from a position of strength as a valued service provider so this should be possible. We definitely need to re-position our business. We have strengths in business and systems strategy which are not perceived by the client. We also have an arm of the business which is capable of not only advising on Business Process Re-engineering (BPR), but can also translate BPR solutions into Information Technology enabled ways of working. The client is not aware of this and has no perception of how this part of our business could potentially help them with the drive to reduce costs.

The next step is to translate these emerging goals into SMART Objectives and then to build a Plan of Action.

WHICH TOOLS TO USE?

There is no rule as to which of these tools a firm should use in its Key Client and Crown Jewels Client planning processes. Depending on the value and complexity of the client, it may be useful to use all three: they all add a different dimension to the analysis of the relationship with the client. For more simple Key Clients we stress again that a 'top of the head' set of Objectives and Plan of Action may well be OK – and is definitely better than nothing.

There is just one scenario to avoid: we should not make the leap from using no tools to the introduction of three simultaneously.

CLIENT INFORMATION

There are three different types of information we may choose to gather about our clients. These are:

1. *Base Information.* This is simple data that we probably need in order to either produce internal statistics or to have a fundamental understanding of the client's business.
2. *Thinking Information.* This is information we gather about the client and the client's organisation which could stimulate our thinking about their business and help us in the exploration of new areas of work or the formulation of appropriate Objectives and Plans of Action.
3. *Our Information.* This is information purely for internal use. It enables anyone in our firm (for instance, a new member of the Client Service Team) to understand what has happened in the past, what the situation is today, and who, from our firm, is involved.

Ground rules

We will examine the different information fields we may choose to build using these three main headings. For this exercise we will put the following ground rules into place.

* *This is purely a menu.* Any firm or practice area can choose what it deems important and what it sees as information for the sake of information.
* *There is no right amount of information to hold.* More is not necessarily better unless it stimulates better management of the client relationship and more profitable fee income.

- *A clear decision must be made as to what information is required about each Key Client and what is not.* We have seen the following happen on numerous occasions. Originally it is decided (for valid reasons) to seek information about Key Clients in a great number of areas. When implementation sags, the professionals complain that the task is too onerous (or perhaps it asks too many questions to which they have no answer!). An improvement is suggested. Why don't we simplify the information fields by consolidating them? That will make the whole task smaller, more manageable and simpler.

  We end up with one heading that reads something like the following. 'Client's point in business cycle, critical success factors, business objectives, key strategies, competitive threats and opportunities'. The heading means nothing, but even the most poorly informed professional can now fill in most of the half-page dedicated to this.

  This fudge totally devalues the whole reason for seeking the information in the first place. The aim is not to write down the bits we know about a client, but to stimulate our thinking about what we know and what we don't know. If we don't see value in having a piece of information, don't include it. If we do, then we seek specific input. For instance, if we know our client's objectives but not the strategies to achieve these, let us be clear about what we know and what it may be of value to learn.

- *A (D), a (T) or possibly a (D/T) will follow each information sub-heading.* The (D) signifies that this information could be a field within a database. We may at some point in time wish to analyse the percentage of our business coming from the Leisure sector or from a geographical region. Unless we capture the information in this way from the beginning, this will prove difficult.

  The (T) suggests that the information will be in a textual format. Any search will have to be carried out using key words.

  The (D/T) which we use occasionally suggests that the information could be structured in such a way as to make it retrievable from a database, but alternatively it may be recorded in a textual format.

  In this menu we will offer an explanation as to why this information may be of value in Key Client planning – if the explanation is not immediately apparent.

To give context to our example we will position ourselves as an Information Technology (IT) consultancy.

Base Information

- *Client name (D).*
- *Address (D).*
- *Main telephone number (D).*
- *Main fax number (D).*
- *Main e-mail address (D).*
- *Website address (D).*
- *Details of parent organisation (D).*

- *Industry (D).*
- *Industry Sector (D).* With both Industry and Industry Sector we have a choice of using Standard Industry Classification (SIC) codes or of creating our own system of classification, which is more suited to our firm. If our business is so highly diversified that we deal with anyone and everyone as a client, then we may choose to use recognised SIC codes. If there is more focus in our business, then the detail of SIC codes may not be appropriate and we will be better served by creating our own industry classifications.
- *Our relationship classification (D).* Is this a Valued Client, a Key Client or a Crown Jewels Client? We may want other classifications based on other factors. This enables us to analyse fee income and fee income type by type of client served.
- *Geography and location of the client (D).* Many clients will have more than one office or plant. We may want to have details of satellite operations on file.
- *Organisation structure – with structure chart (T).* If a client has numerous offices or geographically remote operations this diagram should show the relationship between the various parts of the business. Which companies belong to which divisions? This chart does not go into the details of key position holders.
- *The client's products and services (T).*
- *Senior Management Structure – with organisation charts (D/T).* Key position holders and their titles can be listed, along with their contact details. This is useful information to include in a database. Additionally it is invaluable to have a copy of the latest organisational structure. Who reports to whom? Does the Director of IT have direct line reporting to the MD or does he report in through the FD?

Thinking Information

External factors

- *Industry pressures and issues.*
  - Who are the client's established competitors and what particular threats do they pose? (T)
  - Who are the new entrants into the client's marketplace and what is their competitive positioning? (T)
  - Who are the client's customers and what is happening in their market that may affect our client? (T)
  - Who are the main suppliers to our client and what effect can they have on our client's business in the future? (T)
  - What are the 'left field' alternatives to our client's business that may prove a challenge or competitive threat in the future? (T)
- *External pressures and issues.*
  - What pressures or opportunities may our client face that are brought about by changing social expectations or mores? (T)
  - What technological changes are likely to have an impact on our client in the future? (T)
  - What environmental issues may affect our client? (T)

- – What is the future economic outlook and what effect will that have on our client and their business? (T)
- – Are there any likely political changes, either in this country or in countries where our client has interests, that will have an effect on their business? (T)
- – What impending legislative or regulatory changes are likely to impact our client's business? (T)
- – What effect will the changing nature of Europe have on our client? (T)
- *Critical success factors.*
  - – What are the recognised critical success factors for businesses operating in our client's marketplace and how does our client match these benchmarks? (T)
- *Takeovers/mergers.*
  - – What is the takeover and merger activity in our client's marketplace? How is this likely to develop in the future? Is our client likely to acquire or is our client a possible acquisition target? What opportunities or threats does this create? (T)
- *Position in their marketplace.*
  - – As a summary of the above, how is our client positioned in relation to their marketplace in the future? (T)

The client's business

- *Point in the business cycle (T).* The classic business cycle has four stages. These are start-up, growth, maturity and decline. If we can identify where our client is in the business cycle this may suggest services and capabilities which are likely to be of value to the client.
- *Financial performance (T).* It may be of value to understand various dimensions of a client's financial performance – perhaps over a three- to five-year period in order that trends can be analysed. Is turnover growing? If so, by how much? What about gross margins? Are these increasing or decreasing? Are profits on the increase or decrease? What is the gearing of the client? What is the trend regarding working capital? How much of its profits is the client re-investing in the development and growth of its business?

  We may want this type of information in absolute terms or we may want it benchmarked against the client's closest competitors. A growth rate of 12 per cent per annum is less impressive in a market where most players are growing at over 20 per cent.

  The sort of financial information that is of greatest interest to us will depend on the type of advisory services we provide. What is bad news for the client can be good news for us. Declining margins on core products may be a positive indicator for a consultancy with the expertise to develop new products with the aid of advanced technologies.

- *Future objectives (T).* Reading the client's Report and Accounts may be helpful in creating a high-level view of what the client is seeking to achieve over the next year – or five years. However, there is likely to be little detail in this source of information. Such documents are also read by competitors. There is no substitute for talking directly with senior people within our clients and finding out from them their objectives – and their dreams! – for their organisations. If we have a clear view of our client's objectives, we can position every suggestion we make and every piece of work we propose for, as a facilitating action aimed toward achieving the corporate goals.

- *Future strategy (T)*. An objective of a client could be to increase market share by 10 per cent in the next three years. This tells us what the client wishes to achieve, but gives no insight into how they believe the objective will be met. They may develop the product line, they may increase their channels to market, and they may increase production volume, lower their unit costs, reduce prices and gain market share in this manner. Alternatively they may go on the acquisition trail and buy the additional market share. Knowing the intended strategy of our clients again helps us to position our services congruently.

- *Image in their market (T)*. How do their customers and competitors regard our client? What is their perception? What image is our client trying to create in the market through positioning and advertising and promotional activities? Are there differences between our client's perception of their image and the market's perception? If so, does this present us with opportunities?

- *Strengths and weaknesses (T)*. By looking in depth at the external factors affecting a client's business we should have a good perspective of the opportunities and threats that they face. We may also find it useful to consider the factors within the business that represent its strengths and weaknesses. The strengths may give us insight into how the client organisation will behave in its market in the future. Usually businesses play to their strengths. Understanding the weaknesses can give us insights into what causes senior managers to lose sleep. Any ideas or improvements we can suggest here will find a receptive audience.

IT environment

In this sub-section of information we are seeking more specific data which could particularly affect the type of services we provide. If we were carrying out this exercise for a law firm the heading would be 'legal environment'. If we specialised in corporate finance work the heading would be 'Corporate finance environment' – and so on. This example is for an IT consultancy.

- *IT strategy (T)*. In achieving the corporate goals and implementing the planned strategies, what is the role of IT and how will it be positioned to support the overall strategy?

- *Communications strategy (T)*. Is this an integrated part of the IT strategy or not? If not, what is the strategy for building electronic communications in support of the IT strategy?

- *Technology base (T/D)*. What hardware and software does the organisation use currently? How is this integrated and configured?

- *Age of systems (T)*. Perhaps this should be called 'fitness of systems'. A system may be quite old but it could be perfectly functional. On the other hand a quite new system may be failing to deliver the business benefits anticipated.

- *Current hardware, software, communications and soft services suppliers (T/D)*. Who currently supplies the client? What is the nature and quality of the relationship these organisations have with the client?

- *Development projects – today and future (T)*. What projects is the client currently working on and what projects are likely to be implemented in the future in order to carry through the IT strategy in line with the business strategy?
- *Levels of in-house IT capability (T)*. An outside adviser provides support to a client because the client does not have the capacity in-house or does not have enough of the capacity in-house. It is usually valuable to know what expertise the client has within their business. We can therefore position our services as support – not duplication or a direct competitive threat.
- *Past, current or future use of other consultants and IT advisers (T)*.

Buying Process
- *Budgets (T)*.
  - What IT budgets does the client have?
  - What budgets does the client have for consultancy support?
  - What training budgets does the client have?
  - What do each of these budgets cover? (e.g. does the training budget cover venue and subsistence costs as well as the costs of training?).
  - Are there thresholds of authority or single project limits on any of these budgets?
  - Who has ownership of these budgets?
- *Tendering process (T)*.
  - Does the client have a specified tendering process? If so, how does this work?
- *Decision-making process (T)*.
  - Is there a defined process?
  - If so, what is it?
  - Who gets involved?
  - When do they get involved – at what stage?
  - What are these people's criteria for supporting one proposal over another?
- *Typical bases of decision (T)*.
  - What criteria does this client usually use to arrive at a decision as to who to use for IT consultancy support?
  - Is the decision usually driven by familiarity with current providers, the cost of the solution, the nationality of the solution or the perceived resilience and robustness of the 'best' solution?
- *Paper trail (T)*. After the client makes a decision to use us, do we understand the client's paper trail? Understanding the paper trail means that the work is fully agreed and confirmed, that we have our invoices accepted, that these are tied into the client's purchasing system, that variation orders can be raised easily (if necessary) and that we will be paid in a timely fashion.

Buying personnel

We could seek to find the following information.

*   *Titles and positions (D)*.
*   *Level of authority and influence (D)*.
*   *How they perceive us (D)*. Level of authority and influence and how they perceive us can be combined and shown visually as suggested earlier in this chapter under the heading of 'Relationship Analysis Model'.
*   *Position on the ideas adoption curve (D) (Figure 7.3)*. People within our clients' populations can be categorised by analysing the way they adopt new technology, new ways of working, or new ideas. These sub-divisions are often illustrated using a normal distribution curve (bell curve).

    We classify a very small proportion of the population as Innovators. They like new ideas just because they are new. With regard to information technology, for instance, they will try new products and technologies even though they may have to carry out considerable work to generate any real value from them.

    Next along the curve come Early Adopters. These people are risk-takers because the new idea or new technology is still relatively unproven.

    The Early Adopters are followed by the Early Majority who in turn are followed by the Late Majority. As the name suggests, these two groups form over 80 per cent of the population. Finally, there is small group called the Laggards who are carried kicking and screaming to adopt twentieth-century ideas as the rest of us are beginning life in the twenty-first century.

We can consider each of the people who may be involved in relation to decisions

Figure 7.3: The Ideas Adoption Curve: identifying the propensity of individuals to adopt new ideas and approaches

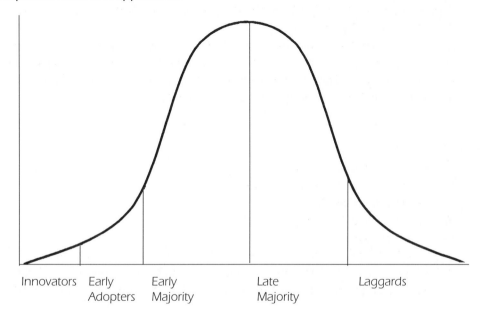

| Innovators | Early Adopters | Early Majority | Late Majority | Laggards |

about using our firm from this perspective. Where do they typically sit on the ideas adoption curve? If we think from this perspective we may gain greater insight into how we best position our proposals to gain the buy-in of different individuals.

Client organisations may outwardly state that they seek creative and imaginative ideas, but organisations do not make decisions – people do. If we find that the people we deal with are typically in the Late Majority, they will welcome solid proof, a proven track record and sound references. On the other hand, this sort of assurance has considerably less value and appeal to someone who is an Early Adopter.

- *Critical success factors (T)*. Here we are not referring to the critical success factors for the client organisation. Instead we are seeking to understand the critical success factors for each individual who could have an influence on using our firm in the future. If we know how their performance is judged (i.e. *their* critical success factors) then once again we have more insight for positioning our proposals more appealingly.
- *Bases of decision (T)*. Just as there may be bases of decision for the organisation, the people involved in making the decisions may have their own personal bases of decision. The individual's position on the ideas adoption curve and their personal critical success factors will probably heavily influence these bases of decision. These are not the only factors, however, and all manner of personal preferences and prejudices may shape a person's decision-making criteria. This is potentially vital information.
- *Background (T)*. Where a person has come from will affect the way they make decisions and the direction of these decisions. We must all have experienced this. A new decision-maker, who has had a poor experience of our firm at some time in her past life with another organisation, will bring the image of this experience with her. What were the people we are dealing with today doing in their past lives?
- *Interests (D)*. Knowing a person's interests can be valuable. If a person within the client's organisation is keen on motor racing, then a hospitality event held at the British Grand Prix will, in all probability, be well received. An invitation to the opera, on the other hand, may not create the same positive effect.

Competition
- *Competitors used in the past (D)*.
- *Services and capabilities utilised (D/T)*.
- *History of relationship (T)*.
- *Satisfaction of client with competitors' work (T)*.
- *Penetration of client by competitors (T)*.
- *Levels and volume of resources employed by competition when working with client (T)*.
- *Reverse RPI score (D)*. Earlier in this chapter, one of the Key Client planning tools we examined was the Relationship Protection Index. If our score was extremely

high on this index it would be a foolhardy competitor who would invest much time in trying to win that part of our work with a client that was well protected. We would be similarly foolhardy to attack a part of a competitor's relationship with a client if this relationship was well buttressed against attack.

A reverse RPI score seeks to ascertain reasonably objectively how well the competitor has protected their incumbency in a particular type of work, from our attack. All sound strategy is based on fighting battles which can be won.

OUR INFORMATION

As part of our Key Client file we may hold a set of information we define as 'our information'. This could include:

- *Who is involved in the Client Service Team (D)*
  - Name
  - Title
  - Location
  - Contact numbers
  - Role within the team
  - Type of work done for client
- *Previous work carried out for client (D)*
  - Type of projects
  - Value
  - Who was involved
  - Summary of results
- *Current work and projects being carried out for client (D)*
  - Type of work
  - Value
  - Who is involved
  - Current status of project
- *Past and current contacts with client (T).* Nothing destroys a professional firm's credibility more quickly than to demonstrate to a client that the right hand does not know what the left hand is doing. If the client has to say, 'I have given this information to two of your people on separate occasions in the last three weeks', it is clear that our internal information system is not what it should be. If we even run the risk of this happening then there is room for improvement. For complex clients in particular, where we may have many parts of our firm in touch with many parts of their business, we need an information system that lets everyone know what is the latest state of play.

The role of information technology

Knowing what we have done for a client in the past and knowing exactly where we are with today's projects potentially requires links into our billing systems and practice management systems.

Having an up-to-the-minute, real-time picture of every outcome of every discussion with all our contacts within a client organisation definitely requires technological support. In the next chapter we will examine the type of support that information technology can supply – helping us to better plan and manage our Key Client relationships.

KEY CLIENT PLANNING – A SUMMARY

- The Key Client plan can be as simple or as detailed as we choose to make it. It is perfectly OK to have very simple plans for some of our Key Clients and more considered plans for strategic or Crown Jewels Clients. We should not try to impose one template across a wide variety of clients. It would be better to agree on three, four or even five levels of 'intricacy'.
- The simplest Key Client plans are one page in length. They contain some base information about the client and then go on to outline what we are seeking to achieve with the client in the next time period (our Objectives) and how we are going to do this (our Plan of Action).
- The core of the most detailed Key Client plans is still our Objectives and Plan of Action.
- However, to aid us in formulating these plans we have at our disposal three key tools (Relationship Protection Index, Relationship Analysis Model and SWOT Analysis).
- Also, sitting behind our plan, we can have a potentially vast store of Thinking Information. The more accurate this information, the better the insights. This should lead to the generation of more focused and creative plans.
- The type and detail of the Key Client plans we wish to construct is our choice. The aim of this chapter is to provide the options. The critical factor is to implement the option (or options) we believe fits our clients most appropriately.
- It is the actions, not the plans, that produce the results.

FIRST STEPS

1. Take one piece of paper. Select one of your Key Clients. Picture in your mind what the relationship with this client would be like in two to three years' time if things go well.

    - What work will you be doing?
    - Who will you be working with?
    - How will the client perceive you and the firm?

    Note down two or three SMART objectives to be achieved within one year that will represent good but achievable progress towards the two to three year vision.

    Note down the three to four key actions you will need to take in the next two months to start towards these objectives. Make sure the action plan is SMART.

    Put these actions in your diary.

2. Take one of the tools in this chapter – RPI, RAM or SWOT – and apply it honestly to one of your Key Clients. Consider the results of your analysis and decide on the two or three specific actions that you will carry out to counter any threat, exploit any opportunity or strengthen the relationship.

    Put these actions in your diary.

    When you have completed these actions use the tool again or use another tool.

3. Select one Key Client and over the next six months embark on a campaign to gather a significant amount of 'Thinking Information' about this client.

    Review the information and see what insights it brings in:

    - How you might develop stronger relationships with this client.
    - How you might help the people in the client's organisation to achieve their objectives by providing new services to them.
    - How your firm might develop its offering to more closely match this client's current and future needs.

    If these insights stimulate ideas for action, put them in your diary.

Chapter 8 **Using Supporting Technology**

The simplest Key Client plan can be committed to one sheet of paper. When this type of Key Client is managed by one person in the firm, and this person also carries out all (or most) of the professional work, there is no reason to have anything more sophisticated than a piece of paper.

However, for many Key Clients, and certainly for Crown Jewels Clients, this simple state of affairs does not exist. The client can be complex, with many divisions and geographical locations. We may deal with some parts of the organisation and not others. We may believe it is valuable to know a vast amount about the client's business. We may have a number of people involved in managing the client. We may have many more different people involved in executing the work. We may believe that it is vital to have an up-to-date understanding of what is going on in the client's business and what the state of play is with regard to the work we are conducting.

In short, a piece of paper will not do. We need to turn to technological support. However, we need to turn in the right direction.

A client of ours spent many thousands of pounds a few years ago investing in a Key Client management system. Frustrated by the lack of support from their central IT function, this part of the firm went out and bought a good package that provided them with far more control over, and information about, their client management processes.

After a period of time it became apparent that there was a problem. Whilst the system provided useful information to those involved in client management and business development, it was yet another island in the sea of systems that the firm was accumulating. Whilst many functions were unique to this system, much data was duplicated and this system could not talk to other elements of the IT infrastructure. In improving their client management processes, this part of the firm had added to the business's overall IT shortcomings.

FUNDAMENTAL DEMANDS ON A KEY CLIENT MANAGEMENT SYSTEM

- The system must integrate with the rest of the firm's IT infrastructure.
- The system should allow (and encourage) all relevant parts of the firm to access, and contribute to, more effective client management and firm-wide communication.

- The system must be technically capable of performing the functions we require of it.

In this chapter we will examine in some detail what we should be considering if we are thinking of selecting and implementing a system to help us with Key Client management.

SPECIFYING A KEY CLIENT MANAGEMENT SYSTEM

The following are some of the criteria we believe that most firms should consider when weighing up a potential system.

- Proven capability.
- Configurability.
- Scalability.
- Hardware and communications compatibility.
- Remote accessibility.
- Accessibility for the Client Service Team.
- Accessibility for the firm's client-facing support people.
- Security.
- Updated, real time, synchronised information.
- The ability to hold both simple and complex data about clients.
- The ability to manage very complex clients.
- The facility to construct Key Client plans.
- Links to correspondence files.
- A basis for a marketing activity database.
- A summary of all client activity.
- A means of flagging future contacts.
- A means of managing new selling opportunities.
- A summary of work in the pipeline.
- A source of sales (and other) statistics.

Proven capability

The first question that could be raised is: 'Should we try to find a system in the marketplace or should we build one ourselves?' A few years ago this question may have given rise to a healthy two-sided debate. Today the question is redundant. The application of technology to managing the client interface followed decades after the application of technology to managing a business's finances. Decades later it may be – but this technology certainly exists today. There is a whole cadre of products and solutions addressing this application. Originally these were grouped under the generic term Sales Force Automation (SFA).

First exposure to this terminology may feel like a cold shower to professionals. Sales Force Automation does not sound as though it has much to do with the handling of Key Clients. It sounds as though it is something designed for soap powder salespeople to check if they are making enough calls per day. Indeed the very first SFA products were designed to perform such functions. SFA products have, over the years, developed in sophistication and functionality to the point where the terminology Sales Force Automation is an inadequate description. Enter Customer (or Client) Relationship Management systems (CRM).

The majority of systems that are available originate from the US. There is nothing inherently wrong in this, but it does mean that the sale of the product and any adaptation and configuration is left in the hands of local distributors. Typically they can configure the basic product up to a point – but beyond that point we have to accept any inherent product limitations.

What does that tell us? It suggests two things:

1. We should select a system that is proven in the professional services arena. Previous applications do not have to be exact replicas of our business but they have to contain the same elements of application. For instance, if we were involved in Human Resources Consultancy, a system which had been successfully implemented twice in an Engineering Consultancy environment would probably be worth close inspection. However, a system that had been successfully implemented 50 times in a consumer durables environment but never in a professional services situation would be of dubious value.
2. If possible, we should find a system where the people who configure it have total access to all of the design parameters and therefore have no limitations on how the system can be configured to our particular situation. Ideally we would be dealing with the originator of the system. In the worst-case scenario we would be dealing with an accredited value-added reseller who is able to convince us of their technical capability and support and who has the confidence of the system designers to change even some of the most core functions of the system.

Configurability

We may want our system to contain additional information parameters about our clients. These may not be part of the system the vendor is trying to sell us. We may want the facility to change, or add to the database fields at some point in the future. Can we? Can we do it ourselves or do we need someone to do it for us? If so, how much is this likely to cost? We may decide we need new reports in future. Can this be done? Can it be done easily?

There are two dimensions to configurability – today and the future.

Configurability today

When, in our minds, we design the ideal Key Client management system for today, we should always take expert advice from people who have experience in converting these ideas into systems. A client of ours had the great idea of storing all incoming correspondence by scanning it and keeping it with the rest of the client information and correspondence. An expert advised our client that this was technically possible but it required a vast amount of disk storage space. We should listen to such advice.

If, however, we are being told that all of our ideas are flawed and that we would be better off with the proven core system, we may reach the conclusion that the system is not easily configurable and that someone is trying to shoehorn our application into their solution.

Configurability for the future

However much we try to design a system that is 'future proof' there is no such thing. Our clients will change, our business environment will change and the demands on our system will change. We will find features of our system that are redundant even though we originally believed them to be indispensable. We will find gaps in the system – gaps we can't at a later date imagine how we left – and we will want to reconfigure part of the system.

Can it be done? Is it possible that one of our own people can do some, or all, of this work? Do we need to bring the system designers back in? What could be the likely time and financial parameters for such interventions?

We need to be comfortable that any system we choose is sufficiently configurable both today and in the future.

Scalability

The Key Client management system we will implement tomorrow may be for one practice area, which consists of twenty people. If, in a year's time, we decided to include all of the other departments in this office (80 additional people), could this be done and how easy would it be? What will be the effect on the system and the way it performs if we multiply the number of users by five? What will be the likely costs associated with this?

What if we decide to roll the system out to our other four offices? Repeat these questions again for the scenario where, in three years' time, we acquire, or merge with, another firm of similar size to our own.

We need to be convinced that the system we are thinking of adopting is capable of handling a user base that could be many times larger than the first pilot part of the firm's business.

Hardware and communications compatibility

Our main system has Unix client server architecture. We have workstations and PCs in our offices connected through router-based Ethernet Local Area Networks (LANs). We have a Wide Area Network (WAN) linking all of our sites including the Bolton office. This office was acquired a short time ago and they use networked Apple Macintoshes. The question is: 'Will this system work across all of these hardware platforms and will it run across the network?' Software and communications architectures are increasingly bridging the gaps caused by the existence of different hardware platforms, but it is essential that this issue be checked out at the earliest possible stage.

Remote accessibility

Many professionals spend more time than ever before away from their offices. We work with professional services clients whose people do not have their own office – or desk: they hot-desk!

Professionals who hot-desk or work remotely from our offices must also be able to have access to the Key Client management system. The professional may need information when he is staying in a hotel or when he is in front of the client. There are different ways of achieving this – the physical contact with the central system can be made by wire or it can be wireless.

Laptops with dial-up modems are commonplace today. This means that if there is a telephone socket available, contact can be made with the central system (subject to the system being supported by remote LAN access).

The alternative is a more recent technology. Just as we have wireless digital mobile voice communications, we also have wireless mobile data communications. This enables the professional to link into the central system from any location where he can pick up a signal – in the same way that a digital mobile telephone has connectivity.

Whether this is a requirement of the system will depend on the likely usage by the professionals concerned. It is easy to say that in most situations a professional will have access to a phone socket – so why would he need mobile communications? However, one could also use that argument in respect of voice communication – and then observe everywhere the pervasiveness of mobile phones.

There are also two basic choices as to how the system can be presented in a remote access situation. These are:

1. A direct link into the central system. The remote device would dial into the central server.
2. A link into the firm's intranet. In this instance the Key Client management system is incorporated as a fundamental component of the firm's intranet.

Early systems were all designed around having direct remote access into the central server on which the system was held. However, access to the system via an intranet connection is becoming more common. One simple benefit of this form of remote access is that call charges are less. Another benefit is that all of the remote users of the system do not have to have the system loaded onto their PCs and laptops. This is time-consuming and is rarely a one-off task as upgrades and changes have to be implemented across all devices using the system.

Whatever the choice of technology, the system must allow easy and speedy access to users who may find themselves outside of the firm's office environment.

Accessibility for the Client Service Team

All people who have responsibility for managing the client relationship or for carrying out work with the client must have access to the system. These people need to update Key Client plans. They need to enter file notes relating to discussions with the client. They need to amend information – and so on.

It was not so long ago that Key Client management systems had an administrator. Among this person's other duties was the collection of scraps of paper from the people who dealt with the client, and the updating of the Key Client plan or the Key Client database. The system lived on this person's desk.

Desktop and laptop PCs are the tools of most professionals today. It will only be a few years before we are able to state that these devices (or their descendants) are the tools of *all* professionals.

Regardless of technology, any professional, following any form of contact with a client, should note the details of this contact. This may take the form of a letter to the client, a note to colleagues or a reminder note that will be logged on the client file. The professional who leaves the contact to memory is either one of the few gifted people who has perfect recall of everything, or is a person prepared to take unnecessary risks with the relationship. This we consider unprofessional behaviour.

Technology makes it possible to save this note in electronic format without having to route the process through a central administrator. No extra effort is involved. A letter can be sent to the client and a copy stored on the client's electronic file. An e-mail can be sent to colleagues and a copy again stored on the client's file, or a note can be made and stored similarly. Any professional who is dealing with the client should then have access to updated client file information.

Accessibility for the firm's client-facing support people

The information that is contained in Key Client files should be a firm-wide asset. The information may be valuable for people in our marketing group. It would be useful for our credit control people. It would provide a basis for other parts of the firm that have a wish to work with other parts of the client with whom we do not have involvement today.

Perhaps the senior partner is to meet with someone from one of our Key Clients in two days' time. He can go into the system and find out what we have been doing, who we are talking to, what the live issues are, what problems we may have encountered in the recent past and where we are with current work. He can pull off hard copy of the information that will be particularly valuable and he can update himself on the train on his way home. Briefing meetings, which eat up valuable professional time, can be reduced substantially and when they do occur they will be conducted by informed people who are focusing on key issues identified from the Key Client file.

Any system should allow (and encourage) all relevant parts of the firm to access, and contribute to, more effective client management and firm-wide communication.

Security

This is always something of a trade-off. How can a system provide easy accessibility to all, and perfect security? Answer – it cannot. However, that is not to say that we should not consider reasonable security precautions.

There may be parts of the Key Client plan that need to be password protected and are only accessible to a nominated group of people. There may be parts of the Key Client database that are 'read only' for many people in the firm. In other words, they can access the information but they cannot change it, delete it or write over it in any way. It should be impossible for casual staff (who have no need of the information contained in the Key Client system) to find a way of gaining access. Passwords should be changed regularly.

All of this is good housekeeping. However, if there is someone who is a member of the Key Client service team who wishes to copy all the files and take them with him when he leaves the firm, there is little that one can do about this. (Of course we should spell out in the terms of the Contract of Employment that this constitutes theft of the firm's property and will be treated accordingly.) Before the advent of computers, such people with ill intent used photocopiers, and before this pen and paper.

We should be comfortable that the system we choose can provide a level of security commensurate with the levels of accessibility we are also seeking to provide.

Updated, real time, synchronised information

Imagine a professional who works from home and spends little time in the office – or a professional who spends a lot of time away working with international clients. These people, if they are users of the Key Client management system, will be entering information on to their laptops or home-based PCs. At the same time, other people in other offices will also be entering information about clients. It is easy to understand how, with a large client, it is possible to end up with disparate local versions of the same client file. Any system we are considering must be able to overcome this potential problem. There are two ways of doing this.

First, there can be an automatic download function. This means that when a remote user has cause to log on to the central server, the first function that is carried out is a downloading of recently loaded information from the server to the remote device. The reverse also occurs. Any data entered on the device since the last log-on contact, is downloaded to the central server. This ensures that everyone logging on to the central server has the latest version of data available on any client whose file is maintained electronically.

We have heard some complaints about this type of facility; these nearly always centre on the time taken for the data transfer. As one professional said to us recently, 'I just wanted to find one simple piece of information. I had to wait twenty minutes for the updating process to finish before I could begin.'

The second way is built around having the Key Client management system as an integral part of the firm's intranet. As the system is not loaded onto the user's remote device, the user has to directly access the intranet to enter information. The user is, in effect, entering this information directly on to the main server.

Whatever form of technology is used, it is usually important that the file held at the central location is a replica of the data being used by others in remote offices or those using remote devices.

The ability to hold both simple and complex data about clients

Most databases used currently by professional firms carry very simple information – similar to the Base Information fields referred to in the previous chapter. For those prospective clients where we have done little work in trying to define our selection criteria (explained in detail in Chapter 2 of *Creating New Clients*) this may be sufficient data to hold. After all, these 'suspects' may receive mailings and invitations from us and little more. An address, a telephone number, an industry classification code and a name of someone whom we believe is the best contact could be enough.

For a Crown Jewels Client this is hopelessly short of the mark.

In the past, the answer has nearly always been to build another system. Sometimes this took the form of a paper-based Key Client file. Sometimes the local PC whizz-kid built his own new database format. This activity, happening in one department, could be replicated across a large firm. In a few years databases abound – all designed to do different things. No one is willing to concede his system, as the other proposed systems do not provide the precise type of information required by that department or that person.

The requirement for a database of clients was originally (in most firms) driven by the finance function. Having client details on computer meant that billing could be computer based and the sales ledger could be maintained electronically. Beyond the base details of the client (and possibly a link to the time-sheet system) there was no need for further sophistication of the client database.

In the previous chapter we have given a menu of information which may be valuable to hold on any Key or Crown Jewels Client. All of these information fields are unlikely to be required by any firm. However, for complex and strategic client relationships, the firm's core database must be designed so that the information considered to be important in managing important clients can be captured. This potentially means a lot of data fields and a lot of data.

In most firms there is a need for a role reversal with regard to the firm's database. The people who manage the clients should specify what they want to know about their most important clients – what they would ideally like to be held on an electronic database. The people in the finance and administration functions should then work off this. In the past it has always been the other way round.

In practice the client-facing professionals should involve their finance and administration support to ensure that all interested parties are able to extract the information which is of value to their function.

The firm should have one database. It must be capable of holding information in the numerous fields that could be required for a Crown Jewels Client. It should also be possible to enter the most simple Base Information about a client or prospective client, and nothing more.

The ability to manage very complex clients

Some of our competitors include their client list in their brochures – presumably to impress prospective clients. We often have a chuckle at the organisations that claim they deal with 'Shell'. Shell is not an entity that a consultancy carries out work for. Shell is a multitude of organisations and business divisions, located all around the world. Consultants invariably carry out work for a discreet part of the Shell organisation that has a defined decision-making authority.

We suppose it looks much more impressive to claim a working relationship with Bloggins International rather than The Post Room Division of the Administration Department of Bloggins Scotland Limited.

Returning to our Shell analogy; we cannot think of Shell in the same way as we think of a client organisation that has one business, located out of one head office location and run by one management team.

We are not suggesting that we build our Key Client management system on the assumption that a division of Shell will become a client of ours tomorrow. We are suggesting that a system that assumes that all clients are simple structures with no overlap will probably not, over time, meet the needs of most professionals.

For instance, Jim Smith may be the Financial Director of Norgon UK. He could also be the Financial Director of the parent company – Norgon Inc. He may hold the position of board member for the Engineering Employers Federation. If we examine the data held on Norgon UK, a good system will allow us to pick up immediately that Jim Smith has other interests in other parts of our client (or non-client) base.

We should be able to look up a major conglomerate on our database and then drill down to find the daughter companies with whom we carry out work. We should equally be able to look up those parts of the organisation where we are carrying out approach activities with the aim of finding work, or those parts where we have never carried out any proactive business development activities.

We need to think about how complex our clients are (or may become) and ensure that any system we employ can deal with, and provide meaningful information from, this level of complexity.

The facility to construct Key Client plans

If we choose to use any, or all, of the Key Client planning tools outlined in the previous chapter, these should be provided in electronic format. This gives anyone involved with the client a snapshot of the factors that comprise our RPI and how we score against these factors. It provides a quick glance at the Relationship Analysis Model – who we know and where we position them. It provides an analysis of how we view the strengths, weaknesses, opportunities and threats in respect of our relationship with the client.

Most importantly, from these tools and from the Thinking Information we have gathered on our client, we can construct Objectives and Plans for Action. As we suggested in Chapter 7, it should be possible to view these in a textual format and, in the case of Plans for Action, in a visual format or representation. The right electronic Key Client management system will allow us to do this.

Links to correspondence files

If we are looking up information on a client and we see that a proposal has been sent to the client a month ago, our system should allow us to readily drop into the part of our system where we store correspondence. Similarly, if we are in the client file and we wish to send a letter to the client, we should be able to call up our word processing package. We type the letter, and the address and greeting are integrated from the Key Client file. The switching to and fro from the Key Client file to stored correspondence and to our word processing package should appear to be seamless.

A basis for a marketing activity database

So far we have considered a Key Client system as a mechanism to help us manage the relationships with the clients we have today. However, as we stressed earlier, the firm should have only one database. This database should also be the source of all information about our marketing and promotional activities aimed at prospective clients. Not only should the database provide the raw material of names and addresses for mailing purposes, it should also act as the summary information for the marketing and promotional activities which have been carried out in the past.

For instance, I may have an interest in a non-client organisation. If I look up our database I will probably only find base information on this organisation (to be expected). However, I should be able to get a summary of all the promotional activity which has been directed toward this prospective client in the past. I should be able to find out which mailshots we have posted and when, which newsletters were sent and to whom, and which seminars we have invited people to and who has attended. The system should act as the core source of knowledge of all activities directed toward prospective clients.

A summary of all client activity

If it is helpful to know what effort we have expended in marketing to non-clients, it is obvious that it will be at least as helpful to have an up-to-date picture of the activities we have carried out with Key Clients.

Too often clients conclude that their advisers find it impossible to co-ordinate the right hand with the left. Clients see effort duplicated. They pass on a piece of information to one person within their firm of advisers and it is clear in the next meeting that this person has not passed the information on to his colleagues who would also find the input useful. The client has to waste time and effort repeating the message.

Recently a client of ours told of a situation where a partner rang one of their valued clients and invited him to lunch. The valued client declined as he was already occupied on the day in question – attending a function with another of our client's partners. Embarrassment! Worse than this is the conclusion that a client may draw from this type of incident. The client may think, 'If they can't communicate between themselves on something as simple as this, how do they handle a really complex and challenging piece of work!?'

We stated earlier that a summary of all client contacts should be kept. This is fundamental. Our Key Client management system should allow us to see at a glance what activities (meetings, phone calls, client service reviews, entertainment activities) have been carried out with whom within our Key Clients.

Sitting behind this abbreviated data should be some form of correspondence or file note. If I discover that someone within a client has had a telephone contact with one of my colleagues two months ago, I should be able to find an electronic file note which gives me some indication of what the discussion was about. If the detail of this note is insufficient, I may decide to speak with my colleague to obtain more information.

On the other hand, the file note may contain enough of an indication of what the previous contact was about. In this case I can ring the person I intended and begin that discussion from a well-informed position. I also have not had to trouble my colleague for more information. Sounds like Utopia – but does it also sound like hard work and the need for a lot of self-discipline? We will look further into this in Chapter 9.

A means of flagging future contacts

If a good system can help us to look backwards and know what has happened in the past, it should also help us to manage our activities in the future. We may speak with a client who says, 'We will definitely need to talk together on the help we need for the MARS programme, but not until the senior management team have appointed their respective management bodies. That's going to take three months, so why don't you give it another month after that then give me a call.'

The best, most professional advisers have found their own systems to ensure this follow-up call happens and happens on time. We are astounded, however, by some of the people whom we meet whose diary management does not extend to coping satisfactorily with this type of situation. Clients are neglected, astute competitors are knocking at the door and 'captive' business is lost. If it is 'mandatory' commonsense practice to record in brief format every client contact, then it is a simple extension of this practice to note when the next contact should take place.

A good Key Client management system will flag up the activities that need to be carried out as they occur in the future.

A means of managing new selling opportunities

In Chapter 5 we examined how we should track the progress of our selling activities when opportunities are found within our existing clients. Very often these opportunities can be competitive and we need to manage our approach strategy in such a way that we maximise our chances of success and at the same time minimise our competitors' chances.

Opportunity Management has three main phases. The first phase is built around a template which tells us where we are in the sales process, what we know, what we don't know and what actions we have already implemented. The second phase is the formulation of a plan that will take our selling process forward and put us (or keep us) in the position of favourites to win the new work. The third phase is the implementation of this plan. Depending on the length of time available for the client's buying process, we may see two or more iterations of this overall process.

It is useful to have this analysis of our sales position and the subsequent plan available electronically, particularly if the selling opportunity is carried out by a number of people.

A good Key Client management system will provide this picture of each of the selling opportunities within a Key Client. Bear in mind that in a large client there may be several new business opportunities being pursued at the same time. Some people may be involved in only one of these opportunities. Others may be involved in a number. The ability of computers to organise data can, in a good system, allow us to see where we are with a number of concurrent business development situations, each of which can carry distinct identification codes or tags.

A summary of work 'in the pipeline'

Any system that collects information must also be a potential source of reports. If we are tracking all of the major business development opportunities available within our Key and Crown Jewels Clients (and why not our Key Prospects?) then it is possible to produce a report that shows the state of play and health of business 'in the pipeline'.

The report can show the clients with whom we are engaged in discussions. It can show the value of the work we are discussing, the likely decision date on the work in question, the dates or period when the work should be carried out, the estimated chance of success and possibly the next actions which need to take place to increase our chances of winning.

Managing partners know what has been invoiced in the past. They have a good idea of the work that is being carried out today. They have a reasonable handle on work in progress (driven in the UK by the taxation laws if nothing else!). Few have any real picture of what is round the corner.

Business is great if everybody is extremely busy. That is a picture of today. That is what we call rowing-boat management (all our information is about where we have come from. We have no data on where we are going. We are facing the wrong way). Most managing partners have experienced the cyclical nature of professional services work. The very fact that we are extremely busy today may mean that we are not putting enough effort into developing new opportunities within our clients. When we finish the hump of work we find that the opportunity cupboard is bare. This is not even management: this is acting as a passive observer of events – the passenger in the rowing boat.

Someone in the practice should be demanding to know what the future holds. Someone should insist on piloting a canoe – not sitting back in the rowing boat. The foremost piece of information this person should be examining is the 'business in the pipeline' summary. A good Key Client management system should provide this.

A source of sales (and other) statistics

Knowing the state of health of business 'in the pipeline' is critical to managing the future health of the firm, and therefore reports analysing the quantity and quality of the pipeline are essential. However, these are by no means the only statistics that we can draw from our information technology systems. We may want to know how much work we have carried out for a client over a period of years. We may want to know what percentage of work comes from a certain market sector. We may want to analyse the changing product or service mix within our client base. We may need to find out the levels of work in progress for a complex client with numerous discreet decision-making points. How do we do this?

One alternative would be to log all this sort of information against each of the clients on our Key Client management system. However, this would usually involve a total duplication of effort. Much of this information already exists within other computer programs. Some of it may reside on our time recording system and some on our billing system. Some firms have invested in totally integrated practice management systems and this information is to be found there. In the twenty-first century re-recording information is akin to returning to the quill pen.

Our Key Client management system must therefore be capable of 'speaking', and integrating, with the other information systems within the firm that hold important information about our clients.

The aim must be to have a Key Client management system which is a central part of a totally integrated information technology system. It must not be a stand-alone, isolated database run by the marketing department. A good Key Client management system will be capable of the type of integration to which we refer.

Clearly the implementation of such a system is not a matter of installing a few disks containing software. The provider of such a system has to spend time with us to understand what our current systems do and don't provide. They must understand what we want our Key Client management system to deliver. They must understand our working practices.

They must then be able to configure their core product – which we must already be convinced has the basic capability and functionality to meet our particular specification.

VIEWS OF A CRM SYSTEMS SPECIALIST

During the work on this chapter we have had the opportunity of liaising with Peter Smith who runs a consultancy called IT & Sales. As an independent consultant, Peter is the author of *The Guide to the Successful Selection & Implementation of Sales and Marketing Software*. which he published himself in 1999. This is an excellent guide that we would recommend to anyone thinking about selecting and implementing a Key Client management system. It takes the reader through a logical twelve-step process that begins with an initial exploratory discussion involving interested parties. The second of these steps is the construction of a cost/benefit analysis and business case. We know of a number of firms who have considered Key Client management systems, only to reject the concept at a very early stage for being 'too expensive'. We cannot recall in any of these cases the situation where the proponents were able to justify their support for a Key Client management system through a fully justified cost/benefit argument.

With Peter's permission we reproduce two excerpts from his publication. These are:

1. A comparison of 'traditional' client management database software functionality compared to the functionality of 'twenty-first-century' software.
2. A 'management summary' of the main factors to consider at the outset when thinking of embarking on a Key Client management systems project.

We have reproduced this list of potential functionality in full. We accept that most professional services firms would have limited use for the software functionality that provides information on (for instance) third-party management. However, the full list does provide an insight into the art of the possible.

Table 8.1: Database software functionality comparisons

Function	'Traditional' software	'Twenty-first-century' software
Contact tracking	One job at one company.	Multiple profiles.
	You may or may not be able to profile the contact, e.g. interests = golf.	Multiple roles at different organisations.
		Events attended record.
		History automatically transfers to new position.
		Tracks involvement in different sales opportunities.
		Preferred address for correspondence.
		Language of choice.
		Male or female. (Foreign names do not always tell you.)
		Job type (not just title).
		Details of projects involved with past and present.
		E-mail address and mobile phone number
Organisations	One entry per postal address.	Group hierarchies, the ability to view a whole organisation and view the relationships between group companies.

Table 8.1 (continued)

Function	'Traditional' software	'Twenty-first-century' software
Mailing, target marketing	Search and sort on a variety of criteria. Link to word processing. UK address and salutation formats.	Worldwide address and salutation formats. Links to UK postcode address file. Link to fax server and e-mail for mailshots. Import and export files from third parties, e.g. your mailing house. The use of profiles on contacts and companies for laser guided target marketing. An automated campaign of mailings, i.e. a series of different mailings to the same targets. Links to external data sets, e.g. financial reports and geo-demographic data. Provides analysis on the success (or otherwise) of your different marketing initiatives.
Activity analysis	A variety of reports available to report on how many calls, meetings, etc.	Activity-based costing, linking costs to actions so you can measure the costs vs the potential profit on a bid. Monitoring activity over time, e.g. tracking that a first meeting has been followed up in an agreed timescale. Analysing activities against best-practice targets, benchmarking your performance against the best company in a similar non-competitive market.
Enquiry handling	Capturing the enquiry. Sending out standard letters, logging the enquiry and setting up a follow-up action.	Profiling the enquiry so you can automatically prioritise the follow-up actions and involve the people in your organisation with the right skills and experience. Automating the response to send a series of letters to the enquirer. Automatically setting follow-up actions to the correct person.

Table 8.1 (continued)

Function	'Traditional' software	'Twenty-first-century' software
Opportunity management	Tracking the progress of a sales opportunity from enquiry to prospect to sale or loss. Providing a sales forecast report.	Proving analysis of the per cent chance of winning a bid via a detailed bid scoring system. Holding all the details of the history of the bid. Providing a range of sales forecast reports including a factored forecast. Tracking the costs of a bid. Providing a database of resources for the bid and automatically finding the most appropriate reference site(s). Providing reports on your sales pipeline and representing your sales methodology, whether an internal system or a proprietary system.
Communications	Support for networks. Probably support for physically remote users.	Sophisticated and automated support for physically remote users. Replicated databases worldwide. The use of the Internet for remote users. The ability to have different views of the database at different group offices.

Six areas that may or may not be supported by 'traditional' software but should be supported by 'twenty-first-century' software:

Function	'Traditional' software	'Twenty-first-century' software
Events marketing	?	Automated systems for following up acceptances to events and re-contacting those people who have not responded.
Customer care	?	Service calls, market research, complaint handling, enquiries. Systems to support ISO9000.
Computer/ telephone integration (CTI)	?	Creating a list and automatically dialling it. Incoming caller identification automatically brings up their record before you answer. The ability to transfer a call and the record to another user.

Table 8.1 (continued)

Function	'Traditional' software	'Twenty-first-century' software
Interface to corporate systems	?	Links to accounts, time recording, project management and e-mail. A common ID for a company across all systems using SQL database tables.
Marketing through third-party channels	?	The ability to effectively manage links with third parties and track the end user. The ability to avoid double counting on a sales forecast when two business partners are bidding for the same deal.
Internet access	?	The ability to link to the Internet for remote access to the system and for capturing details from potential clients who have browsed your Web page and expressed an interest.

'Management summary' of the main factors to consider at the outset when thinking of embarking on a Key Client management systems project

- Calculate the Return On Investment for the project.
- Determine, publicise and monitor the benefits you expect from the project.
- Do not rush and do not linger. The system is going to bring benefits, so whilst avoiding rushing into mistakes get on with it before the people and the conditions change beneath you.
- Those responsible for client management and marketing must own the overall responsibility for the project.
- An executive who reports into or is on the Board has to be on the project team.
- Do not 'do it yourself' – the time and cost involved in in-house development will be prohibitive.
- Allocate sensible money for the project. If you are expecting serious benefits then you cannot expect to achieve them on a shoestring budget.
- Allocate specific amounts of money for training and implementation. Double whatever number you have just thought of.
- Budget for ever. There is an ongoing need to support this project year on year.
- Do not automate inadequate systems. Take the opportunity to improve your systems, otherwise you will just get to hell faster.
- Do not import out-of-date, inadequate or duplicated data.
- Prioritise the order in which you are going to implement the system.

- Spend as much money as you can possibly afford on getting the best technology.
- Don't raise a purchase order, agree a contract to purchase with acceptance criteria.
- Ensure your system can be expanded and amended, supports open standards and can integrate to other systems in your business.
- Decide what percentage of your total criteria you will accept. The cost of achieving above 80 per cent may be more than the benefit.
- Stage the project implementation. Stage 1 of a project means you are committed. Pilot means you are prepared to throw it away if it is unsuccessful.
- Ensure the system supports your communications requirements, e.g. remote workers.
- Establish the specification for Stage 1 and do not let it expand. Put everything else into a box marked 'Possibilities for Stage 2'.
- The system has to enhance and replicate your processes. You should not have to change to fit the system.

Sharing the firm's knowledge

Problem

Imagine a professional on his way to a client review meeting. He has prepared for this meeting reasonably well. The last client service team meeting was productive and he believes he understands all of the issues related to the work in hand and projects about to be undertaken. On these subjects the professional feels comfortable and confident.

However, the professional has also been charged with the responsibility of developing new business opportunities from this client. What should he try to sell them? Considering this question on the way to the meeting, the professional is very uncertain and lacks confidence. He knows that in theory he should know more about the client's business and market sector. He knows that he should understand better his firm's other capabilities. That's fine in theory, but he is a top fee-earner. His expertise is in high demand and 80 per cent of his time is spent engaged in executing client work. He doesn't have time!

As he travels to the client's premises the sorts of questions that run around in his mind are:

- What are the latest factors affecting this client's marketplace?
- Even if I have some knowledge of these factors, what are the exact implications for clients like the one I am about to meet?
- How do these implications affect the type of person I am about to meet?
- How should I explore the potential issues? What questions should I ask?
- If I find something that the client is looking for assistance with, will my firm have the capability to help?
- What could I convincingly tell the client about my firm's capability in this area?
- Who are the experts in my firm?
- What unique capabilities may my firm have to offer over and above other firms that may also be able to help?

- Who have we done such work for in the past and who would be willing to provide us with referrals?
- If I suggest that the client should take the issue further with my firm, what are the weaknesses my firm has in this area, which the client may question? If these weaknesses are probed, what should my answers be?
- Who are the likely competitors and how does their capability compare to ours?

Too many questions and not enough definitive answers. The image of credibility and competence that the professional displays while discussing the client's perception of past and present work has a high chance of evaporating if the professional strays into this discussion area. This is a minefield. The search for selling opportunities will have to wait until next time. Unfortunately next time there is still no opportunity to prepare for this part of the meeting.

We have referred to these problems earlier in this publication. In Chapter 5 we looked at why some professionals felt inhibited about selling their services through a perceived lack of knowledge about the client's business and the market dynamics issues affecting the client. In Chapter 6 we identified that one of the four key reasons for poor cross-selling was a lack of knowledge about the firm's full range of products, services and capabilities.

Quite clearly, if professionals are to sell effectively, these knowledge gaps have to filled. Given the nature of professional work, they have to be filled speedily and efficiently. Additionally, the knowledge must be current.

Solution

Systems exist today that make access to corporate knowledge instant. As we write, this genre of software has not been exactly categorised. The best description we have heard is the term *knowledge sharing*. Unlike CRM systems, where there are a multitude of competing products, this arena appears to be less crowded. We have spent time examining WisdomWare, which is probably the leading product in this market. Its capabilities are very impressive.

Let us return to our professional pondering on the problems of how to seek out opportunities for additional work from the client with whom he is about to carry out a client review. Our professional arrives at the client's premises half an hour early. He opens up his laptop and enters his firm's knowledge-sharing package. He looks up his client's sector. He gets immediate information on the latest market dynamics. He is presented with a list of four potential issues that could affect businesses such as his client's. He takes the first issue and is presented with three potential implications that may affect the person he is about to meet.

He clicks once and he is presented with five key questions he should ask to ascertain the effect of this issue on his client.

What if this *is* an issue and the client is seeking help? How can his firm help? Another click and a summary of the firm's solutions and capabilities is presented. The experts in the firm are identified so the professional can quickly find the right people in the firm to talk to – without wasting his, and others' time in unproductive calls. The professional can call the relevant people from his mobile phone or send an e-mail.

Clients for whom the firm has carried out similar work and who are willing to act as referral sources are named. Competitors he is likely to meet when proposing for this type of work are highlighted. The firm's strengths and weaknesses in doing this type of work, and when vying for it against others, are identified. Where the firm has weaknesses that may be questioned, he is presented with best suggested answers to such questions.

The half-hour is well used. The professional identifies two areas that he wants to explore with the client. He feels very confident that if opportunities are found in these two areas, he has the knowledge to deal with them professionally. If he really gets stuck in the meeting, or if the client asks him a question that he has not been able to prepare for, he can refer to his hand-held computer.

Sounds like a fairy story? Sounds like something that will never happen in professional services firms? If you believe that, then consider these two points.

1. You are out shopping and you enter a catalogue store. You look through the catalogue and select two items. You walk to the cashier who enters your two items into her terminal. She tells you that one of the items is in stock and you know from previous experience that you will have it in your hand within two minutes. She tells you that the other item is not in stock in this store, but there is stock at another store twenty miles away. They will transfer this item from the other store and you can pick it up the next day if that is what you choose.

    This experience is mundane and it is something we have experienced for years. Junior checkout clerks, paid a fraction of a professional's salary, have access to a huge volume of knowledge about their company's business. These businesses know that if they are going to serve their customers well, they must be able to tell the customers about the products they can buy. The concept has been around a long time.

2. If knowledge sharing has a value in business, what sort of organisations should have the greatest interest in the technology that delivers this? The answer is simple – businesses that base their whole value proposition on the knowledge they have within their organisation and the knowledge they deliver to their clients. In short – professional services firms. The concept has been around a long time. We are looking at a new application.

A NEW ROLE FOR MARKETING

If the marketing department of a professional services firm exists in order to facilitate the development of business, then we see marketing taking on a new role in the future. Selling and business development is primarily in the hands of the professional staff in most firms. Professionals mostly recognise that this is a part of their role. However, many are not confident. In large part this is due to a perceived lack of skills and a lack of knowledge. Skills can be developed through training, but we believe that in future the marketing department should be providing the knowledge bullets for professionals to fire.

Traditional ways of disseminating knowledge are of no use. Attending briefings and lectures is time-consuming. Books, manuals and directories are out of date before they are printed. Besides, different professionals in different circumstances want different configurations of the same information. Only a technology-based solution can provide this. If marketing really want to equip professionals with the ammunition to be able to sell the firm's current services, then they have to provide the knowledge that professionals require.

SUMMARY

In Chapter 1 we stated that a lack of available information technology was not, today, a cogent reason for poor Key Client management practices. In this chapter we have endeavoured to outline some of the key factors a professional services firm may wish to consider when contemplating the technology that could support all aspects of Key Client management.

As outlined at the beginning of this chapter, we believe that the three fundamental issues to bear in mind are:

1. The systems must integrate with the rest of the firm's IT infrastructure.
2. The systems should allow (and encourage) all relevant parts of the firm to access and contribute to more effective client management, firm-wide communication and knowledge sharing.
3. The system must be technically capable of performing the functions required of it.

FIRST STEPS

1. If you have no influence on the IT spend of your firm don't wait for the firm to get its act together – do what you can with paper and a diary.

2. If you are senior but have little interest or understanding of IT solutions, show this chapter to someone responsible for systems within the firm and ask them to compare their plans to our recommendations.

3. If you have high influence and some responsibility for introducing computerised systems in this area, what are you waiting for? Put the project team together today. Work through the cost/benefit exercise. This is an opportunity to use technology to gain an advantage over your competitors.

Section 4 **Issues for the Firm**

Chapter 9 **Managing Key Client Relationships**

CHARACTERISTICS OF KEY CLIENTS

In Chapter 2 we made the point that there can be a number of ways to define a Key Client or a Crown Jewels Client. A Key Client could be a small client that produces low fee income but is of significant value to the firm in other ways. Mostly, however, these types of clients will be in the minority when a firm decides which of its clients are 'Key'.

The majority will display one or (more likely) a number of the following characteristics:

- The client will produce (or have the capacity to produce) large fee income volume.
- The client will be large and complex.
- The client will utilise (or will have the capacity to utilise) more than one practice area from our firm.
- The client will utilise (or will have the capacity to utilise) more than one product, service or capability from the practice areas of our firm that do business with the client today.
- The firm will work for (or have the capacity to work for) more than one division or department of the client's organisation.

THE NEED FOR CLIENT SERVICE TEAMS

The processes of Key Client planning and Key Client management can be applied to any size or type of client. A sole practitioner managing 'his' clients can apply the thinking and the tools we have outlined in earlier chapters. However, because of the characteristics of most Key Clients, Key Client management is not usually a sole practitioner pursuit. In most instances Key Client management is a team activity.

In the great majority of Key Client situations, many parts of our business are dealing with (or attempting to deal with) many parts of the client's organisation. Left unmanaged (or left to be managed by an unco-ordinated bunch of sole practitioners) we have a potential recipe for disaster as the client quickly realises that she is dealing with a firm where the left hand does not know what the right hand is doing. There is a need therefore for Key Client teams (or client service teams as we will refer to them) to be formed.

Many professional firms tell us they have already worked this one out: they have client service teams. The next thing to find out is how well these teams work within these firms. Senior partners may claim they work very well, but whenever we have spoken with team members who participate in these teams, we usually get very different feedback.

CLIENT SERVICE TEAMS – THE REALITY

The kinds of things we hear about are:

- Individual parts of the firm still going off and 'doing their own thing' with the client, working on the philosophy that it is better to ask for forgiveness rather than ask for permission.
- Client service team meetings that are continually cancelled.
- Client service team meetings that only occur due to some form of compliance pressure.
- Junior substitutes fielded at client service team meetings in place of the partners and senior managers who are meant to participate.
- Meetings dominated by the partner who 'owns' the client – telling all other team members what they must not do in relation to the client in question.
- Meetings that are an interminable catalogue of 'what I've been doing with this client over the last six months' stories.
- Meetings that focus purely on what has happened with this client over the past and spend no time discussing and agreeing a plan for the future.

These behaviours reflect the common experience of professionals involved in client service teams. Understandably, faced by such experience, many professionals are not committed to the client service teams to which they are allocated. Some we know are waiting for this latest fad to pass so they can go back to the way they did things previously. Client service teams add a layer of complexity that the firm does not need, they burn up time and they achieve very little or nothing – so why have them?

Teams or groups?

Where firms experience the behaviours referred to above, we would argue that they do not have client service teams: they have client service groups. Are we just playing with words? Is this just an exercise in semantics?

There are a number of fundamental differences between a team and a group. Professional firms want to have client service teams. They want to present a co-ordinated, united, planned, professional approach to their Key Clients, but because they either don't know how to form a team or they have not spent any time in creating a real team, they often fall well short of this goal.

Most client service teams become an internally focused group who meet on sporadic re-scheduled occasions in order to be able to put a tick in the Key Client management compliance box.

DEFINING A TEAM

So how do we know whether we have real client service teams or client service groups? For a team to exist there are four fundamental criteria that have to be met:

1. The team must have a common and united vision.
2. The team must have agreed goals and objectives that reflect the vision.
3. The team must be interdependent.
4. The team members must have defined roles and responsibilities.

Until these four criteria are met, a team does not exist – what we have is a group. Most client service teams we have met are really groups.

Common experience

Vision

Not untypically, the reasons for a client service team's existence are to minimise expensive mistakes and to maximise the amount of business obtained from the client; not exactly uplifting and motivating visions.

Objectives

Objectives and goals very often do not exist. These are dangerous because one may fail to achieve them. If we say we will achieve 30 per cent more fee income from a Key Client next year and we fail to achieve this objective, then someone may try to hold us accountable. Better not have objectives – far too risky! Let's stick to vague statements such as 'Maximising any fee income opportunities'.

Interdependency

The different people and departments represented in the team's meetings operate in a totally independent way with the client – and use the meetings to communicate what they have done. With some luck these activities can be spun to appear as though they were part of a bigger co-ordinated plan.

Roles and responsibilities

Team members do have defined roles and responsibilities. After all, they represent their parts of the firm. So what does having roles and responsibilities in a team context mean? It means that over and above representing one's part of the firm, a team member should also be making specific contributions to the effective functioning and maintenance of the team.

Fifteen people in a minibus, all going to the same destination, being driven by the same driver, do not make a team.

Fifteen members of a football team on a minibus not only have a common direction, they have a clear mission, common goals, defined roles and, to be successful, are dependent on each other.

Professionals' experiences of teamwork

In training workshops, when we are focusing on client service team formation and management, we often ask the participating professionals to tell us about the best team they have belonged to and to describe why that was.

Stories come from people's pasts – their time in another company, their time at university, even their time in childhood. Stories can also relate to a professional's current life outside work. The themes though are the same. The stories are about a band of people who were all striving to achieve the same thing – united in vision and spirit. They describe goals that had to be met – and were. They talk about real synergy – about people all pulling for each other. A failure of any one individual could have meant failure for the team – so people went out of their way to support and help one another. They describe individuals who made heroic contributions and filled difficult and demanding roles within the team. They describe other things as well, but a collection of these stories always includes the four fundamental criteria that have to be present for a successful team to exist.

BUILDING THE KEY CRITERIA INTO A CLIENT SERVICE TEAM

The lesson is clear. If we have a desire to create real client service *teams*, then we must create the conditions and environment in which a team can be founded.

Let us take the example of a client service team in an IT consultancy.

Shared vision

The vision of the client service team could be: 'Through their experience of our professional work and relationship management, no division of Client X will ever make a significant decision about IT without referring to us.'

Now there's a vision! Difficult to achieve and difficult to maintain, but a vision that anyone in the team can hold in their minds.

A team member can visualise a group of senior managers from Client X discussing a strategic part of their business. These managers conclude that a part of an important way forward for their business involves their information systems. One of the managers says, 'We'd better get our consultancy's thinking on this one first of all.' Everyone around the table nods: no discussion; no dissenting voices. That's how things work in Client X. This is not complacency in action: this is the epitome of the result of a very successfully managed client relationship.

Agreed goals and objectives

In Chapter 7 we examined the type of objectives that could be part of a Key Client plan. All the messages of Chapter 7 hold good. However, the most important objectives will all be tied back to the central vision the consultancy has for this client, and these objectives will be agreed by all of the members of the client service team. Objectives for the client service team could include:

- To deliver the current Distribution project on time and with minimum disruption (measured by hours downtime) to the client's Logistics division.
- To flag up any unexpected issues in the Distribution project to the client's management team as soon as they are identified, and to present alternative solutions to such issues.
- To discuss with the senior management team of Client X the subject of IT as an enabler to the achievement of their future strategy.
- To have this discussion twice in the next year.
- To present in each discussion at least three ideas that could have significant impact on their use of IT in achieving their business objectives.
- To replicate the 'consultant on-site' situation (achieved in the Manchester facility) in two other locations by the end of the year.
- To win at least one piece of work related to the Client X's potential exploitation of Computer Telephony Integration (CTI) by the end of the year.

The first two objectives are about meeting the client's expectations and being proactive – fundamental to being thought of as 'part of the Client X team'.

The third objective is about positioning our firm as an organisation that goes beyond executing projects in a technically efficient manner. To immediately be thought of as 'our IT people', the senior management team in Client X have to be convinced that our firm instinctively knows what is good for Client X – in the same way that an internal division of the business would.

The fourth objective is again about becoming a part of Client X. On the assumption that the Manchester situation has been a positive experience for both parties, the achievement of this objective will not only make our relationship with Client X even stronger, it will also produce extra fee income.

The fifth objective is not just about winning new income: it is about demonstrating our expertise in an area in which we have never been associated in the past. If we want Client X to think of us whenever there is an IT issue, we need to have demonstrated very wide capability. We must continue to win work in new areas within Client X – minimising potential infiltration by other boutique and niche market competitors.

Interdependency

Our Systems Division could be successful in winning a piece of work in CTI. Our Communications Division could win it. Both scenarios represent possibilities rather than probabilities. The worst-case scenario is where the two divisions make independent approaches and fight each other for a CTI project. This is not make-believe; this has happened in the 'real world'.

If we are really serious about winning a CTI project, we will have to approach these opportunities with a combined team. Some people will come from the Systems Division and some will be drawn from the Communications Division. Success will only happen if people from the two divisions really work together.

The client has to see the approach as totally seamless. If the client sees gaps between the divisions in the selling phase, we will not be appointed: the client will not be prepared to take the risk. The gaps could easily appear during the client's project. No client would willingly expose herself to this type of uncertainty.

An interdependent approach to every aspect of managing the relationship with the client is vital.

Defined roles and responsibilities

Within our IT consultancy's team we have some people who have particular roles. They are:

*   *Alan.* He is the Client X Relationship Manager. Everyone in Client X knows that the ultimate responsibility for the way the relationship works between the consultancy and their company is Alan's.
*   *Barbara.* She is responsible for all aspects of the Logistics project.
*   *Caroline.* She is responsible for the Key Client plan for Client X. She does not formulate it: that is a team effort. However, she records it, she is the guardian of the plan and it is her responsibility to record progress toward objectives.
*   *David.* David is the meetings co-ordinator. He plans all team meetings, pulling relevant agenda items together from any part of the firm that has a contribution to make.
*   *Eric.* Eric is responsible for communications. Among other things this means that Eric has the authority to 'gee up' any person or department not contributing (in a timely manner) information about their activities with the client.

Alan, Barbara, Caroline, David and Eric also have a 'technical' role in the client service team as well, representing their parts of the firm or their technical specialisation. However, their 'team maintenance' roles are particularly important in ensuring that the team functions as a co-ordinated unit.

OTHER REASONS WHY TEAMS DON'T WORK

Having the four fundamental criteria for teamwork in place is vital, but it is not enough. There are other reasons why a client service team may not function optimally. These are:

1. Teams are incompatible with the hierarchical and/or sole practitioner nature of the firm.
2. The most senior people in the firm do not support the concept and role of client service teams.
3. Poor team behaviour proliferates:
    *   Team members lack self-discipline and are unwilling to take responsibility for their actions.
    *   Team members are unwilling to recognise and accept the patterns and processes of teamworking.

- There are no rules as to what constitutes acceptable team behaviour.
- There are no established methods for problem-solving.
- There are no established methods for the team to reach a decision.
- Team members use negative personal communication processes. In meetings for example, they may:
  - arrive late;
  - arrive unprepared;
  - be critical and negative;
  - attack other people personally;
  - attempt to dominate;
  - be constantly judgemental;
  - be prejudiced and/or have closed minds;
  - seek to engage in conflict;
  - interrupt others;
  - be manipulative and political in approach;
  - hide honest opinions but air them later to others in private;
  - mask statements as questions;
  - selectively interpret;
  - use 'You' statements, not 'I' or 'We';
  - agree with everything;
  - opt out and not participate or contribute;
  - express futility, resignation or helplessness;
  - show boredom and don't pay attention;
  - do other distracting work;
  - jump from subject to subject;
  - engage in sub-conversations and mini-meetings;
  - not listen.
4. The team experiences poor leadership.
5. The team has had no training in how to work as a team.

In Chapter 10 we will address the first two of these five points. In the rest of this chapter we will seek to provide ideas and guidance on the following:

- Introducing and achieving team-focused behaviours.
- Leading the client service team.
- Training client service teams in teamworking.

INTRODUCING AND ACHIEVING TEAM-FOCUSED BEHAVIOURS

So often in training workshops, when we give professionals a handout that lists the above negative personal behaviours, people smile and make jokes such as, 'So you've attended one of our meetings then?' Behind the joke is recognition of the reality of team behaviour today – particularly demonstrated when the team meets together.

There is much that can be done to change unhelpful team member behaviour. Much of this is very simple, but nonetheless we know, through introducing our clients to these processes and by using them ourselves over many years, that they are extremely effective.

Help/Hinder

The simplest and most effective process we have seen that changes a group demonstrating poor teamwork into a team that works well together is the creation of a teamworking Help/Hinder list. The Help/Hinder list starts life as a sheet of paper divided down the middle. In one column the team agrees those behaviours which will not be accepted (e.g. it is unacceptable to arrive at a meeting not having carried out interim tasks agreed at the previous meeting). In the other column the team agrees those behaviours that are seen to be positive and supportive of good team process (e.g. if a person has not commented either way on a particular proposal, their opinion will be actively sought).

In firms where poorly behaving teams are prevalent, team members very often complain about others' behaviour – but not in a team meeting situation. If the meeting chairman or the rest of the team do not speak out when people behave in a destructive or unco-operative way, most individuals do not do so either, no matter how peeved they may be by the behaviour they have experienced or witnessed. Poor meeting processes and team behaviour are allowed to persist. The Help/Hinder list gives everyone in the team the legitimate right to 'demand' that all team members behave according to the agreed 'rules' as decided by the whole of the client service team.

For any client service team that is likely to work together for a long period of time and which may meet on a regular basis, 45 minutes or an hour in the first client service team meeting dedicated to agreeing the Help/Hinder list, is an effective investment of time.

The authors' Help/Hinder list (Figure 9.1) is an illustration of how the final product could appear.

Using the AID approach in client service team meetings

The AID (Action, Information or Discussion) approach is a proven method of managing meetings and is particularly effective for meetings that have seven or more participants. We have experience of this format being very successfully employed in meetings involving the active participation of 25 people covering an agenda of over 40 points.

Classifying items on the agenda
- Items for the client service team meeting agenda should be submitted to the meeting organiser or meeting facilitator in advance of the meeting.
- Sponsors of items must correctly define the category of each item and specify the time to be allowed for the item, as accurately as possible.
- The facilitator will either print the agenda in this format or may use flip-charts to display the agenda and how it will be time-managed.
- The sequence for covering items is at the discretion of the facilitator.

Figure 9.1:   The PACE team meeting 'Help/Hinder' list

HELPFUL TO TEAMWORK

Behaviour

Full participation	Focus
Openness to ideas and potential change	Preparation
Broad-brush ideas	All sharing information
Sticking to agreed procedures	Commitments honoured
Turn up – and on time – including after breaks	Active listening – summarising and reflecting
Enthusiasm	KISS
Obviously listening	Creativity
Questioning to understand	No interrupting

Attitudes and Values

Honesty	Valuing group contribution
'Build up' attitude	Focus on the good of the group

Process

Six Hats

HINDER TEAMWORK

Behaviour

Poor timekeeping	Waffling
Too much emotion	Interrupting
Not looking interested	Defensiveness
Negative/bored voice tones	Too much criticism
Too much urgency/lack of patience	Sub meetings/discussions
Thinking of a reply/answer when someone else is speaking	Drifting from the subject
Quick judgement/reaction	Creativity killing
Opinions posing as facts	Too much irony
Lack of planning/preparation	

Attitudes and Values

Lack of consideration for others	Not understanding/no regard for others' work patterns
Intellectual arrogance	Having own/hidden agendas
Devaluing past experience	Paradigms
Seeing past experience as 'the last word'	Not being honest

Process

Wrong participants	Non-scheduled items

The process

Items must be classified as Action, Information or Discussion (AID) or a combination of these.

The way each item is managed is strictly defined as follows.

Action items

For example:

- Items deferred from a previous meeting, requiring a decision.
- Projects to be handed out to individuals or groups.
- New items requiring approval and decision.

Action items should not be allowed to attract any discussion – merely presentation of any information needed and the implementation of an agreed way to determine the action to be taken.

Information items

These are agenda items that impart information, with no requirement for discussion or feedback. For example:

- When the sponsor of an item requires information of a purely factual nature from the team.
- When the sponsor of an item wishes to give information to the team.
- Cameos, demonstrations, research findings, etc.

Pure information items must not be allowed to attract any discussion during the meeting.

Discussion items

For example:

- Items where opinions are sought and exchanged to formulate an approach for future action.
- Items that provide an opportunity for group members to air their thoughts.
- Pure debate.

When managing an item designated for discussion, the facilitator controls the discussion by taking requests to speak from team members and allowing them to contribute in strict chronological order.

Requests to contribute must be made by catching the eye of the facilitator – no one is allowed to interrupt a person who is speaking and no one can arbitrarily 'jump their turn'. However, everyone who has caught the facilitator's eye knows they will have the chance to contribute – and with practice and experience may begin to relax and listen to what their team-mates are saying!

The power of veto on a discussion is possible where an item encroaches directly on an individual's area of responsibility or authority. In a client service team that is working well this should be a rare occurrence.

Discussion/action items

Items where discussion is followed by a decision made at the meeting. The decision could potentially be to defer the item.

Information/discussion items

Information is given to the group and discussed in plenary or in syndicates, but with no immediate action.

Information/discussion/action

This is similar to an Information/Discussion item but a decision for action is required and there must be a mechanism for making a decision.

Better structuring of client service team meetings

To demonstrate some of the ways in which this can be achieved, let us look at an illustration of part of a client service team meeting agenda (Figure 9.2).

Figure 9.2:   Part of a client service team meeting agenda

Agenda for client service team meeting – Client Z – 29 February

	Sponsor	AID	Time
1. Review of actions taken since last meeting		I	15
2. AOB			2
3. Agreement to actions needed to complete current project and ensure client signs off completely satisfied with outcome	JD	D/A	20
4. Decision(s) on how to build closer ties with senior staff in client's Construction Division	PG	D/A	30
5. Decision/implementation of how to recognise success of team involved in Infrastructure Division work	JD	I/D/A	10
6. Updated policy on the use of Associates	TR	I	3

This agenda is very different from many client service team agendas we have seen in the past. The differences are:

1. The agenda employs the AID approach. Each item has a sponsor and a structure for how it will be handled. All items have a time limit so that the meeting does not drag on. The facilitator can cut the subjects once the allotted time has been utilised. It is amazing how focused meetings can become when everyone realises that each item only has a limited time for presentation, discussion and decision.

2. The first item calls everyone to account for actions they were allocated at the previous meeting. A rule the authors have instituted within their own business is as follows. If any person has not carried out the agreed actions allocated to them in the previous meeting he or she must let the rest of the team know in writing of this failure (and the reason for it) at least two days in advance of the meeting. The authors have a short attention span when the subject is excuses.

3. AOB is the second item on the agenda. This is one of the most simple and effective ways of improving team meetings. Everyone has been frustrated at one time or another by a meeting that appears (unusually) to be running to time, only to find that a couple of people have multiple AOBs to add at the end of proceedings.

    The reason for most AOBs is lack of planning, lack of self-discipline or lack of consideration for others – none of which are conducive to good teamwork. By having AOBs at the beginning of the meeting the facilitator can decide if the item will be included or not. If the meeting is to finish by a deadline this means that most AOBs will not make the meeting agenda, no matter who submits them. If the facilitator does decide to include these items they are put onto the agenda with an AID format and time limit. The facilitator decides where these items fit into the meeting plan.

    The authors have extended this process one stage further: they no longer allow AOB items.

4. All the agenda items have a purpose that is clear to team members before they arrive at the meeting. Items 3, 4 and 5 could read:
    *   Current project.
    *   Better relationships with Construction Division.
    *   Infrastructure Division success.

    On most agendas that is how these items would appear. By taking a few seconds and spelling out what the item is about and what the objective of the item is, team members come to the meeting with a very clear expectation of the subject matter. They also have had the opportunity to consider their thoughts on these subjects.

5. There is no place on the agenda for reports on how the different parts of the firm are progressing with their client work and client relationships. These would be Information items. In fact there are few pure Information items on the agenda.

    As we enter the twenty-first century it is bizarre that some people still consider meetings an effective way of communicating information. In many client service team meetings we have seen, more than 80 per cent of the meeting has been dedicated to people letting others know 'what they've been up to'. Great for the ego, but in firms that are meant to sell their time this is incredibly inefficient. No wonder many professionals see client service team meetings as a waste of time.

In some firms we work with they are attempting to eliminate most types of Information subjects within meetings. The reasons for this are:

- Not all Information subjects are relevant to some of the meeting participants.
- A lot of time is wasted while everyone listens to the background to an Information item.
- More time is spent as individuals ask questions to clarify some of the information in more detail.
- Some of the questions asked and answers provided have little or no relevance to some participants, who become bored and switch off.
- Having developed an understanding of the reason for the item, some people realise that they require information and that this is only available outside of the meeting.
- Notwithstanding the previous point, the vast majority of these types of items still continue with discussion following the presentation of the information! Conjecture, guesses, hunches and feelings substitute for facts and information. (Facts shouldn't get in the way of a good discussion!)
- There are far better ways of distributing much of this information, e.g. printed reports, published statistics, memos, e-mail.
- If Information is to be the basis of a Discussion or an Action point, it is better that people have had time to absorb the information rather than to discuss the subject with no thinking time or be asked to come to conclusions with no opportunity to reflect on the data.

To take Information subjects off the agenda of client service team meetings requires certain disciplines.

- Anyone who has information on any subjects that appear on the team meeting agenda should circulate this information before the meeting takes place.
- Agendas have to be circulated to all participants well in advance – certainly not distributed as team members enter the meeting room.
- It is a condition of the meeting that everyone who is attending must be fully briefed through studying the background information. It is not acceptable to catch up on background reading once the meeting is under way and thus ignore colleagues who are speaking.

6. The one Information item on the agenda (Item 6) is a simple one-way communication of policy: it is not for discussion or debate. The relevant information should be communicated in three minutes.

All of these ideas work and will improve client service team meetings. The more of these ideas that a firm adopts, the more productive their meetings will become in the future.

Using the Six Thinking Hats

The most powerful process we have ever worked with to generate productive discussions in meetings is Edward de Bono's Six Thinking Hats. The Six Thinking Hats framework is extremely simple and very practical.

Most meetings involve a lot of discussion. Mrs A raises a point in a meeting. Mr B disagrees with a part of Mrs A's point and makes his own point. Miss C has a view completely at odds with Mr B's and says so in an emotive way. Miss D, an advocate of Mr B's perspective, inputs her thoughts – partially fact and partially opinion. Before we know it we have a healthy 'discussion' in progress, or potentially a full-blown argument.

This is nothing new. This is typical of Western thinking and behaviour and, according to de Bono, evolves from the processes of argument and critical thinking identified and promoted originally by Socrates, Plato and Aristotle.

Maybe it is them we have to blame for meetings that degenerate into circular arguments and consequently overrun by hours.

If we analyse many of these involved discussions we may find that there is much 'point and counterpoint'. In the worst cases the different people engaged in the 'discussion' will forget about trying to prove their point and will focus their efforts on trying to disprove the other point of view. This is based on the assumption that if one perspective is shown to be 'wrong' then the opposite must be 'right'. A little reflection shows this to be very weak thinking.

Despite this, this type of discussion and argument is common. The courts work in precisely this way, the aim being to discredit the other side's case. Is this the reason law firms find it difficult to engage in productive client service team meetings?

In business, this type of thinking and behaviour should be thrown away. The argument system is negative and lacks constructive and creative energy. Synthesising both points of view does not produce a stream of new alternatives and, while people are focused on defending their point of view and attacking others, there is no time or space to seek better ideas.

The Six Thinking Hats is a framework and a discipline that eliminates adversarial thinking and discussion in meetings, replacing this with what is known as 'parallel thinking'.

An immediate reaction to this approach could be a concern that a meeting using this process may fail to examine critically the points, ideas and thoughts that participants put forward. There could be a fear that groupthink will become the norm or that everyone will just agree in order to be nice to one another. Not true. The Six Thinking Hats ensures that *everyone* looks for the flaws in any proposition or idea that the team may consider. Positive, critical challenge is built into the process.

Another immediate reaction can be that a framework like this may make meetings mechanical and not allow people to express their feelings. Not true again. When using Six Thinking Hats there is a place for feelings and emotions, and everyone is encouraged to express how they feel.

In addition there is time and space created for the generation of new ideas and for constructive thinking about the client and the client relationship.

The use of Six Thinking Hats reduces conflict, saves time and makes client service team meetings more positive, creative and constructive.

LEADING THE CLIENT SERVICE TEAM

So often we find that the client service team leader is the same person as the individual regarded as the 'client owner'. For example, in a Big 5 accountancy firm, a major company that has been an audit client for many years may typically have the audit partner as the client service team leader.

We have seen the situation where this person takes on this role driven by a negative motivation. The partner concerned may seek to use the position of client service team leader as a method of keeping the rest of the firm's practice areas in check. If these other practice areas can be kept out of the client or only allowed to operate in areas of low-risk work, then the audit fee can be protected for years to come. Any suggestions that practice areas could be proactive in approaching the client are met with responses such as 'They are focused on other priorities', and 'Now is not the right time.' In fact for these clients there is never a right time as the most powerful partner in the client service team uses the client service team to his own ends.

Clearly, the appointment of such a person to lead a client service team is anathema to the whole concept of teamworking. However, the appointment of 'the most senior person' is the most common criterion that firms use to select a client service team leader. Firms associate (or confuse) leadership with position and hierarchy. We will examine this from a values perspective in further depth in the next chapter.

We are not suggesting that the most junior person in the firm should be a client service team leader: the notion is ridiculous. We are saying, however, that the most senior person on the team or the current 'client owner' do not have to be automatically selected as client service team leaders – in fact they may be totally inappropriate for the role.

Leaders or managers?

Perhaps the first thing a firm should do is to decide if they really want a client service team leader. They may be more comfortable with a client service team manager. Semantics again? We believe not. Warren Bennis, Kouzes and Posner, Peter Drucker and many other leading management writers have clearly identified the differentiation between managers and leaders.

Leadership is about doing things that have never been attempted before. To lead means to be at the front – in this case at the front of a client service team, encouraging team members to attempt things they have never done previously.

New objectives and new activities imply risk, and leaders accept risk: they challenge how things have been done in the past. They say, 'Let's try this a completely different way, a way no one has done before.' Some degree of risk is inherent in such behaviour. Leaders accept this and are willing to learn from the mistakes that may be made along the way. Managers, on the other hand, accept the *status quo* and see their role as administering what already exists: they are risk averse. They may be very good imitators, but they are not originators.

Client service team leaders have a vision of how the relationship with the Key Client could look and they are driven to achieve this through the team. They enlist the client service team members by sharing this vision and by appealing to these people's values, interests, hopes and dreams. Managers inherit what has gone before and 'tinker at the edges' seeking low-risk improvements.

Leaders inspire trust by sharing or delegating their power to team members. Managers rely on control mechanisms to keep the client service team in line. Leaders try to be 'people' people as much as they possibly can, whilst managers are 'structures and processes' people. Leaders communicate with the team – it is a genuine two-way dialogue. Managers issue commands.

Leaders set the example for those in the client service team. They behave in ways that are consistent with the behaviours they say they are seeking from everyone involved with the client. If the leader says it is important to respect clients, then he is never heard to make any jokes at a client's expense – no matter how 'inoffensive'. This doesn't mean he lacks a sense of humour: he can be the funniest person in the firm. He just does not direct this humour toward clients and at their expense.

When things are going well and objectives are being met, the client service team manager accepts this as a logical outcome of excellent planning and execution. On the other hand, the client service team leader sees such achievements as the result of efforts made by people. He recognises this. He says 'Well done' to those responsible. He makes recognition public. He rewards people for their contribution and he is not frightened about celebrating the team's achievements.

In short, a client service team leader does the right things. A client service team manager does things right.

We know of firms in which true client service team leaders fit comfortably. We also know of other firms in which such behaviours would be very ill-fitting – even threatening. We are not saying that one way is right and one way is wrong, although we do have a personal preference. What we are saying is this. Every firm must decide how its client management should be handled. Should it be in a 'managed way' or a 'led way'? No firm should confuse the two. Nor should any firm try to convince itself that it has client service team leaders when in fact it has client service team managers.

TRAINING CLIENT SERVICE TEAMS IN TEAMWORKING

It is logical to conclude that if teamworking is so critical to effective Key Client management, there is a case that we should train our professionals to be better team players. Many firms have reached this conclusion and have taken the next step, which is to embark on training that will teach people how to make a more positive contribution in a team environment.

Often this training takes the form of an outdoor teambuilding event. There is a large market in the UK for this type of training and there are many excellent providers. At one end of the spectrum there are extremely testing week-long courses run by tough ex-military types. At the other there are more gentle one- and two-day activities where the perceived threat to life and limb is less.

One of the objectives of a group participating in any of these courses is to learn how to work better as a team in the workplace. In our experience this objective is not often met. People participate in the event, they throw themselves in wholeheartedly and they have a great time, generally speaking. Years later people are still recounting tales of what happened on their teambuilding course. However, when it comes to changes in behaviour, very little finds its way into the workplace.

Don't think for a moment that we are denigrating these types of events: we are not; in fact we love them. In our own business we usually participate in one each year, and we have a great time!

The shortcoming of these courses is that they are designed too well! Let us explain by taking a typical teambuilding event. When the participants arrive, the course leaders explain the overall event and the teams participating are told (or in some cases, choose) what they want to achieve. A team may choose a target score for the whole event. A team may set out to score better than its contemporaries. A team may set out to break the event record. A team may just seek to maximise the fun element.

The teams are then given tasks and challenges. For each of these challenges there is a 'best outcome', and the team works together to achieve this outcome. These challenges are constructed so that individuals working in isolation cannot achieve them: they can only be achieved through people contributing together. People have to carry out different roles within the team to achieve the challenge objective.

Typically a lot of mistakes are made: people do not communicate well, too many want to run the team, some people are left out; a small band breaks off and does their own thing and the team cannot succeed with its strength divided.

Many lessons are quickly learned in how the team can work better together. The course leaders give feedback on the dynamics of the team – what worked and what hindered progress. The team moves on to further challenges and as the event progresses the team usually gets better at working together and producing team-based results. Each challenge successfully overcome is celebrated as another step toward achieving the team's original goal. Good course leaders also constantly remind the participants of their overall aim for the event. People feel positive and gain a sense of achievement.

At the end of the event it is common that participants feel they have learned much and they believe it will help in the way they interact together in the workplace. However, within a few days the real effect has diminished. Why is this?

We need to look at the way the training event was constructed. The team participating in the event had an agreed overarching vision or objective (perhaps to be the most successful team). For each challenge they had a very specific objective (perhaps to achieve a certain outcome in a designated period of time). To succeed in each challenge every individual was reliant on the contribution of the others and every individual had to carry out different elements of the task.

In other words, the event built in the four fundamental criteria needed in order for a team to function: a united vision, common goals and objectives, interdependency, and defined roles and responsibilities. These criteria are usually 'buried' within the event and they are never explicitly examined.

When the participants return to the workplace with a will to be better teamworkers they often return to situations where there is no common and united vision, where there are no agreed goals and objectives and where interdependency is not built into the way people work and operate.

All the excellent lessons about communicating better and offering support and encouragement to others never take root, as the basics for a teamworking environment do not exist. Gradually things go back to how they were in the past and the teambuilding event is remembered as a 'great couple of days in the outdoors'.

Our recommendations are simple. Whatever teambuilding training an organisation chooses to use must, in its earliest stages, get people to realise and recognise the four essential elements that need to be in place for a team to have any chance of operating well. One clear focus for the event should be for the participants to explicitly consider and conclude how these four elements can be imported back into the team situations in which they operate back in the workplace.

When this issue is a fundamental component of the teambuilding training exercise, then the event has a good chance of delivering real value to firms who choose to make such an investment.

SUMMARY

Most Key Clients will demand some form of team-based approach, therefore sound teamworking is essential for us to meet the client's expectations. For a team to have any chance of succeeding it must have a shared vision of what it is trying to achieve with the client in question, specific objectives, and a way of working that is built on people having defined roles and responsibilities but in an environment of interdependency.

On the assumption that these four essential criteria are in place, there are many tools and processes that can be utilised to ensure that the day-to-day working of the team is as effective as possible. Team co-operation and team meetings can be improved immeasurably through the implementation of these tools and processes, and training people in how to work as a team has great value if it is carried out in the way we suggest.

We believe that client service teams work best when they are led, but whether client service teams are managed or led is a matter determined by a firm's culture and way of working.

FIRST STEPS

1. Select a team situation in which you have some influence. Invest some time at the next team meeting in drawing up a Help/Hinder list and work to this list at the next two team meetings.

   Review any effects this new way of working has.

2. Draw up an agenda for your next client service team meeting. Allocate most time to the future and on developing the client relationship.

   Review the success of this approach and develop as necessary.

3. If you are a client service team leader, consider the differences between management and leadership articulated in this chapter. At the next client service team meeting try focusing your energies on leading the team forward rather than controlling what is already in place. If 'revolution' is inappropriate make small changes, see what impact they have, and develop your approach over time.

Chapter 10 **Values and Characteristics in Key Client Management**

Having reached this chapter, there may be many thoughts in the reader's mind. We hope that one of these thoughts is, 'This is not rocket science.' It's not. We would suggest that 'Applied common sense' is closer to the mark. Yet, as we commented at the very opening of the book, really effective Key Client management is a rarely-found practice in our experience within professional firms.

Possible conclusion: most professional firms lack common sense. This would be an insulting conclusion. Most professional firms have brainpower and sensibility in abundance. Our experience tells us that what they lack is a combination of the following:

1. Leadership of the Key Client management process.
2. The motivation and will to put Key Client management practices at the very core of the firm's strategy.
3. A consistent and universally held belief in the value of proactively managing client relationships.

In the first chapter we commented on the first two items. In this final chapter we set out our thoughts on the third of these issues.

LESSONS FROM PORRAS AND COLLINS

In much of the research carried out by Porras and Collins they seek to understand what it is that differentiates a great business from a good business. This research was the basis of their bellwether publication *Built to Last*. One of the conclusions reached by these two authors is that the great businesses have a very clearly defined set of corporate values that underpin everything the organisation sets out to achieve.

The findings of Porras and Collins, amongst others, have stimulated hundreds, if not thousands, of businesses to spend millions of man-hours in an effort to define their values, their core purpose and their long-term objectives. Much of this is done in the misguided belief that, having defined such values and purpose (and then committed these to paper), this is the first step toward greatness. At most it is the first step away from mediocrity.

Typically these efforts at capturing the essence of a business are conducted by the senior management team. That shows real commitment – but misses the fundamental point that Porras and Collins make.

Porras and Collins stress time and again that the values and purpose of a business are *discovered* – they are not created. The reason that some employees greet many mission statements with undisguised cynicism is that they cannot associate their daily experiences with the values and behaviours promoted in the statement. Their daily experience may often be the antithesis of the corporate 'dream'. Not all of these people who react in such a way are mean-spirited, negative, and anti-company; their honest experience does not support the glowing, well-meaning adjectives the senior management team would like to believe describe their business.

Porras and Collins suggest that if a business wants to really understand its core values and core purpose it should bring together a mixed sample of people from all around the company. These people should, between them, have a long experience of the business, and most of them should be drawn from the lower echelons of the organisation. These are the people who, on a day-to-day basis, experience and embody the values of the business. Give them some time together and they will articulate the real values of the business: that is the process of discovering corporate values.

Sounds dangerous? We must all at some time have come across businesses with which we have felt deeply uncomfortable. The behaviour of people may have been in contradiction to our beliefs. The motives they may have expressed to us in an unguarded moment might have made us feel very uneasy. Imagine if a group of average people from such a business sat down to capture the values of such a business. It could read:

- Profit at any cost
- Exploitation of any customer weakness
- Promotion of personal interests above all else
- Knowledge accrual = power
- Divide and rule

If any of us were working within such a business the last thing we would want is this list of values adorning the reception area wall for all visitors to view. Much safer not to embark on such a project – or better still to have the directors create a whitewash values statement.

EMBEDDING CULTURE AND VALUES

How, then, do the values of a business become embedded? Certainly not by writing down a 'wish list'. The values and culture of a business become embedded through the manifest behaviours of the majority of people who work within the firm.

If someone joins the firm who does not share the same values as the vast majority, he or she has two choices. The first choice is to accept the values of the firm and begin to behave in the same way as those all around. The second is to leave and to find a role in a firm that demonstrates values closer to those of the individual.

There is a third way, but this is extremely rare. In the third way the individual is the catalyst for changing the established corporate values in favour of his or her own.

Unless the individual concerned is in a position of extremely high influence and power, this is an unlikely scenario. Even given the conditions of high power and influence, the chances of changing a whole corporate culture and values are remote. A very powerful and charismatic character may succeed if the business concerned is facing a real crisis and people generally accept that dramatic changes are in order. A rare situation, but one that is the subject of folklore (and business books) when it occurs. Michael Edwardes' story of British Leyland, portrayed in the book *Back from the Brink* (1983) is a good example of this rare but fascinating occurrence.

These unusual situations apart, the culture of most firms is continually reinforced over generations. We recruit people whom we believe will be successful in our environment. We bring on board those whom we think will 'fit'. Some try to hire people whom they 'like'. Sometimes we get it wrong and the fit is not a good one. The individual leaves the firm and we look for someone who is better suited to our organisation. We are not saying that this is necessarily right or wrong. This is not a morality judgement: it is a statement of how things work. In some firms this process is explicit (it is in ours!). In some firms it is implicit. Either way the values and culture become reinforced and embedded. This is why it is so difficult to change when we believe change is necessary.

KEY CLIENT MANAGEMENT – TEAMWORK VALUES?

At the beginning of the previous chapter we suggested that Key Client management was, in the main, a team-based activity and not a sole practitioner activity, although the principles can be applied to any client situation that lends itself to a one-on-one relationship. This would imply that if we are to make a success of Key Client management then we must have a significant number of people within the firm who embrace the principles, and embody the practices, of teamworking.

If a team-based approach to working with clients is not common today, how likely is it that this 'new' way of doing things will take root? Again we reiterate that leadership, motivation and reward will have an impact – but they are not enough. We have to assess if the ingrained values of the business are likely to support this way of working.

ASSESSING THE VALUES OF THE FIRM

Even giving a representative group of people the task of delineating the values of the firm may not be the most productive way of assessing the real culture of the business. Such a group could be swayed by a small number who are, for whatever reason, more interested in producing the right result rather than the real result.

We would suggest getting this group of people together and asking them to agree on their answers to the following questions:

- What are the things that one must do to be regarded as successful within the firm?
- What are the things that one must definitely avoid doing within the firm?
- Who are seen to be the most significant people within the firm? Why is this so? What behaviours do these people personify?

- Who are seen as the role models within the firm?
- When looking back at those people who have left because they did not 'fit', what is it that these people did not have?
- What are the 'nice to have' behaviours that many people would like to see in the firm – but no one does anything to enforce?

The rich mix of answers to these questions will determine the real values and culture of the firm. We have worked with professional firms where the distillation of this exercise results in a culture described as:

- Hit one's personal numbers (utilisation, chargeable hours, recovery, etc.).
- Work with the powerful partners and fast-rising associates and avoid the rest if possible.
- Make oneself very visible to these people.
- Be seen to be working long hours (this emulates the role models).
- Carry out interesting work (and leave the dross to the less capable).
- Be seen to be making personal sacrifices (a marriage is particularly significant).

There is no mention of clients or anything about doing great work for them. There is not even any mention of the firm! Certainly there is no mention of working with others with a view to producing the optimum results for the firm and for the client.

We challenged one group who produced answers not dissimilar to the above about the lack of focus on the client. Their reply was 'That's what we meant.' They then spoke of working long hours in the service of the client and of making personal sacrifices in the name of the client. They even claimed that by focusing on work that was personally very interesting they were giving the client the best possible service. The professional was committed to the work, we were told.

We listened. We reflected back on the two hours of discussion and debate that had concluded with general agreement on what was culturally 'good' behaviour within the firm. We concluded that we were dealing with a group who were quite good at post-behavioural rationalisation. In other words, we did not believe them. We figured that if 'That's what they meant', this very intelligent group of individuals would have found some time in the previous two hours to express some form of sentiment in this direction. They had not.

Why wouldn't a firm take the time to assess its real values and culture by undertaking the exercise we have described? There can be only two possible answers:

- The firm sees no value in the exercise.
- The firm would rather not know the answers to the exercise.

The firm sees no value in the exercise

If the firm sees no value in the exercise, this means that those who run the firm are comfortable with the culture and values of the business as they stand today – and who are we to argue against that? We are not leading a movement for cultural uniformity across professional services firms. We are not creating a list of 'good' cultures and 'bad' cultures: our clients will ultimately decide what is good or bad. Whatever 'good' is will be rewarded with increased success in a competitive marketplace. Whatever 'bad' is will result in falling fee income and reduced profitability. The market always decides ultimately.

The firm would rather not know the answers to the exercise

If there is concern about making explicit the less-than-client-focused real values of a firm, this is the ultimate in putting one's head in a bucket of sand. What is really being said by this approach is, 'We know we have a culture that in some ways is not what we would like it to be, but if we make this explicit we will face the task of trying to change the values of the firm. In undertaking this challenge we believe we do not have the leadership/energy/ability/will/motivation/management capacity or whatever, to see the task through to success. Therefore we will avoid the issue and hope that our clients either don't care or don't notice.'

We can understand there are firms very happy with the culture of their business and how that culture sits with their clients and people – and who therefore see no value in 'belly-button gazing'. We cannot understand firms that just simply do not want to face the real world and their real problems.

DETERMINING KEY CHARACTERISTICS

Assuming that we can address the very real issue of leadership of the Key Client management initiative and the issues of motivation, recognition and reward, what sort of people should we be trying to foster within the firm? Who will adapt easily to this client-focused, team-based environment? What sort of people should we be trying to attract into the firm?

Success in recruitment and selection is a cornerstone of success in many businesses – not just professional services firms. After over twenty years of working with all types of companies, the generally poor and *ad hoc* processes that businesses use to select people no longer surprise us. The differences between those organisations that *really* know how to select the best people, and those who think they do, is vast. Unfortunately most businesses put themselves in the former category and scarcely any business classifies itself in the latter.

We have built a very robust model that is designed to help those enlightened businesses who realise that their selection processes could be strengthened and who know they could be better at finding, attracting and hiring the best candidates. The model is based on a few very simple premises. Three of these are:

1. The aim of any selection process is to find the people who can both fulfil the role successfully and also fit in with the values, culture and practices of our business.
2. Suitable individuals will have identifiable characteristics that will deem them as the most appropriate people for our business and for the role to be filled.
3. The selection process has to be designed in order to test for the demonstrable existence of these characteristics.

Quite simple premises really – but a well-composed CV and two interviews won't cut much ice in our recruitment and selection world. One of the fundamental processes that sits behind our approach to selection is the task of determining the key characteristics required of the person (or people) we are seeking. As fundamental as this is, it is a task that is rarely undertaken with any degree of thoroughness. This is hardly surprising, as most people who recruit staff have no methodology or tools with which to carry out this process.

We provide this methodology through a simple but comprehensive model that we have devised. We introduce this to our clients either as part of the training we provide for them or as part of a consultancy project centred on selection process improvement. For most job roles in most organisations the model provides a 'menu' of around 100 characteristics that could affect a person's ability to carry out a particular role and to fit into the firm. These characteristics will fall into one of the following seven areas.

Personality factors

These are virtually unchangeable in an adult. They are a result of inherited genes and long-term conditioning. For instance, a person's need to compete may be high, low or somewhere in the middle, but there is almost no way on earth anyone (including an employer) can change this type of characteristic in a person.

Attitudes

These are partly a result of the personality of the person and the upbringing and experiences the person has had to this point in his or her life. For instance, some people demonstrate high moral courage and will stand up for whatever they believe is right: they have a clear sense of 'right' and 'wrong' no matter what the circumstances. At the other end of the scale we have people who decide what they believe is 'right' and 'wrong' based on the particular circumstances they are facing at the time. They would see themselves as realistic and pragmatic. Others may see them as being unprincipled.

Circumstances and background

The qualifications a person possesses or even whether they live in the right geographical area could be factors in their suitability for a job role.

Knowledge

This is not the same as qualifications. Qualifications normally mean conformance to some examination standards at some time in the past. This is no indication necessarily of a person's true level of knowledge required to carry out the job role on a day-to-day basis. In very technical roles a high level of knowledge is necessary. However, knowledge is 'learnable' – particularly by those who have a high level of motivation to learn and who have the mental ability to take on board and apply learned information.

Aptitudes

We define these as 'born with' skills. They may be improved but it is very difficult to achieve. Take, for instance, analytical ability. It is extremely hard to make genuine lasting improvements (that can be applied to real-life situations) to a person's level of analytical ability. Some natural aptitudes are vital for certain job roles.

Skills

Skills can be learned: this is how they differ from aptitudes. If the job role requires computer skills, any motivated person can improve the level of skill they employ in this aspect of their job.

Habits

Like attitudes, habits are well ingrained and hard to change. Some people are timely in carrying out their work and display great timekeeping: it is the way they behave or the way they have conditioned or disciplined themselves to behave. Others are always late: they are late and their work is late – it is their whole way of life. Timeliness and timekeeping is an example of a habit affecting a person's ability to carry out a role and to fit within the culture of a business.

We have given an example here of a characteristic in each of these seven areas. Examining all 100 is not the purpose of this book.

In theory it is possible to look at the role to be filled and the culture of an organisation and decide on a 1 to 9 scale (normal distribution curve) at which point our ideal candidate for a job role should sit against all of the 100 criteria. Clearly this is not a practical exercise. It is also flawed as it assumes that each characteristic has the same value as the next: again, clearly untrue.

For application in the real world we ask our clients to select up to twenty (maximum) characteristics from our 'menu' that they would seek within an ideal candidate for the particular role they are trying to fill. They are allowed to have a maximum of fifteen (of the twenty) defined as 'primary characteristics'. The balance are referred to as 'secondary characteristics'.

The process then moves forward – defining a selection process that tests for the demonstrable existence of the chosen characteristics.

Characteristics for the professional firm introducing Key Client management practices

If a firm is moving in the direction of Key Client management utilising a mainly team-based approach, we would suggest that ten characteristics (from our menu of 100) could be significant in:

*   determining if our people are likely to adopt such an approach to our clients, or
*   using as some of the characteristics sought in new professional staff joining the firm.

We will also 'stick our neck out' and suggest the level that would be 'ideal' on a 1 to 9 scale.

The ten characteristics are as follows:

Commitment and loyalty

In an environment where success depends on a team working and pulling together, even when things may not be going too well, commitment and loyalty to the team, to the concept of the team-based approach, to the firm and to the clients is essential.

A person with a 1 score on Commitment and Loyalty would display behaviours consistent with being totally self-centred and would base any commitment to the team purely on a pragmatic 'If it's good for me' approach. A 9 score on Commitment and Loyalty produces the ultimate patriot willing to experience any self-sacrifice to help the team succeed.

We would be looking for a score of 7.

Conscientiousness

In the sole practitioner situation, one's conscientiousness (or lack of it) has the ultimate payback to the sole practitioner. If, due to lack of applied conscientiousness to the task, the sole practitioner loses clients (who find other advisers more dedicated to their cause) it is the professional himself who suffers most as a consequence.

This is not the case in a team situation. One person who fails to carry out his part of the work in a detailed and conscientious way can undo the best team. Others may try to cover for the weakness of one less-than-conscientious team member, but ultimately the client will experience a shortcoming in service delivery. The loss of a client in this situation is a loss not to one person but to a group of people.

A 1 score would represent a total lack of concern for delivering what was promised. A 9 would indicate obsessiveness. We would look for a 7 again.

Dependence

As with all of these characteristics, there are two opposite ends to the spectrum. At the 1 end we have total dependence: in other words the person concerned cannot operate without having close contact and support from others. At the 9 end a person's natural way of doing things is to be totally independent – perhaps even maverick.

Many sole practitioners operate more toward this end of the scale: it is what they prefer and enjoy. It is one of the things that motivates them about the role of the professional as they have engineered it or as their firm has defined it.

We would seek neither highly dependent nor highly independent individuals in a team-based environment. Much day-to-day work has to be carried out individually, but team-based activities by definition do not suit the highly independent who become stifled by the restriction of having to consider and think about others.

A score of 5 would be the best fit.

Sensitivity

Insensitive people scoring 1 on our scale are totally immune to criticism and they are impervious to setbacks. Rejection is taken in their stride – in fact they hardly seem to notice it. People who are engaged in constant new business development need a low sensitivity score – possibly a 2 or a 3. They would otherwise become discouraged by the 'failures' that are part of the usual process of winning new clients. High-sensitivity people avoid new business development. They instinctively know they will be badly hurt by rejection of their approach and they will interpret this as personal rejection.

In a team-based environment we would seek people who are at neither end of the spectrum. Insensitives will not listen to criticism and will ignore feedback. Sensitives will be hurt by well-meaning open and honest feedback about their contribution toward the team effort.

Another 5.

Openness

When reviewing the lessons learned from dealing with a Key Client over the preceding year, the 'score 9' open person will suggest that everyone states openly what they think went well and why, and what they think could be improved and how. When the discussion moves on to how things could be improved, the 9 scorer will expect people to be totally honest about each other's contribution. The intent is not to score points and build political position: that is the total antithesis of the values of the very open person and belongs to the mindset of the Machiavellian low scorer in Openness.

Openness is essential in a team-based environment. We would not suggest people who score 9. Their total frankness and lack of diplomacy may in itself cause problems. However, we would welcome someone who scores around 6 or 7.

Generosity

The two poles of this characteristic are 'abundance mentality' (9) and 'scarcity mentality' (1). We have referred to scarcity mentality earlier in this book (see p. 87). Partners who fight off their fellow-professionals from clients more vigorously than they fight off competitors demonstrate this. Their motto is encapsulated in the phrase 'What I have I hold.'

Professionals with abundance mentality don't need to be persuaded that there is more work within their clients for others: they actively seek out this work and just as actively bring in others whom they believe can help. This is not to say they are undiscerning as to whom they introduce into their clients.

Professionals with abundance mentality will carry out a limited piece of work of which they have no previous experience, for no fee. They recognise that the learning experience and the value of the potential follow-up work are worth the investment. On the other hand, professionals with scarcity mentality will insist that they be paid for every minute of work agreed. They will lose the opportunity to a competitor who has a proven track record in that type of work rather than give up one chargeable hour. Teams need members with high Generosity. A score of 8 would be excellent.

Personal organisation and orderliness

Total fastidiousness and attention to detail in respect of every aspect of the team's work is likely to get in the way of the team functioning effectively. On the other hand, most teams do not fail through over-attention to detail. More teams fail because one or more of the members is not disciplined enough to ensure that they have effectively organised, carried through and communicated their part of the team plan.

It is likely that a person scoring highly on conscientiousness will also score well on Personal Organisation and Orderliness. Similarly, a score of 7 would represent our ideal.

Adaptability

Some people work well in a situation where they are dealing with senior people within a client organisation, but they struggle to communicate with junior staff. Similarly some professionals find they fit in easily with clients who represent religious charities but find it difficult to get onto the wavelength of 'barrowboy' traders. In both these examples the professionals concerned lack the ability to be adaptable in their dealings with different types of people. They have a certain persona that translates well to some but less well to others. The trouble is they cannot consciously (or subconsciously) change the persona they project.

A team can consist of a rich mix of people, and the members of a client service team may have reason to communicate with all levels and types of people within the client's organisation – hence there is a need for individuals in the team to demonstrate adaptability.

Of course, wherever possible, the team should organise itself to play to its strengths. Our top technical people should be the main contacts with the client's technical staff and so on. However, the organisation of team roles is made infinitely easier if most of the people in the team can be chameleon-like when called upon to be so.

Highly adaptable people (7 or 8) would represent the ideal, but in the real world we will settle for a 6.

Teamworking

Meredith Belbin has studied the workings of management teams for the last two decades, and the personality characteristics demonstrated by people who fulfil the team roles he has identified are well tested and proven. In our work with management teams we have used Belbin's teamwork questionnaire on numerous occasions and we have found it remarkably accurate in predicting the behaviours of individuals who find themselves working in a team-orientated environment. However, we are mindful of Belbin's conclusion (published in his early work *Management Teams*) that approximately 30 per cent of individuals do not contribute well to, or fit into, a team.

Individuals who are very independent by nature can make a contribution to a team – if they have the desire to do so: they can harness this independence to aid the team. Perhaps they will volunteer to take on the task that calls for a high degree of isolation from the rest of the client service team – but will equally agree to communicate their progress to their colleagues. This is very different from the independent individual who has no interest in making any contribution to a team effort.

The genuine willingness to be a part of, and to contribute to, a team-based approach is essential, and an above-average score is essential. We would suggest the higher the better – but 5 would be an absolute minimum.

Active listening

Of the ten characteristics we have chosen that affect a person's ability to work with, and contribute to a team, this is the only skill we have selected. Active listening is displayed by people who listen so closely to what others are saying they are able to demonstrate their understanding by

- paraphrasing and summarising the message the other person has communicated;
- reflecting the mood or emotion the speaker has communicated (e.g. 'It is very clear that you believe that this situation should not be left as it is but I also sense that you are somewhat unsure as to what steps you should take').

An active listener picks up not just the words that are spoken but also the whole message that is communicated. An active listener pays attention to the choice of words, to the intonation and to the body language (particularly facial expressions) of the speaker. An active listener focuses on the words, the music and the dance and can identify the congruence or incongruence of these. Moreover, an active listener then feeds this understanding back to the speaker.

Active listening is the most powerful of personal communication techniques. Nothing demonstrates better to us that what we have said has been interesting, valuable and listened-to, than the summaries and reflections provided by a skilled active listener.

Because active listening is an essential interpersonal skill in any situation (within the client service team or in communication with clients) we would love to have people with a score of 9 involved in a team. However, people with this level of skill are extremely rare, so any score above average would be a real bonus.

Not a question of good or bad – a question of different characteristics for different strategies

It is not unusual that once people have compared themselves (or others in their firm) to the above set of characteristics they may become somewhat defensive. 'Are you saying our people are no good? – because if you are, how is it we have done so well in growing our business over the last five years!'

We are certainly not setting ourselves up as judge and jury over what is defined as 'good behaviour' and what on the other hand is 'bad behaviour'. All we are saying is that if a firm chooses to go down the route of managing its Key Clients and Crown Jewels Clients in a more proactive way, this may involve a move away from an historically sole-practitioner way of working to more of a team-based approach. If this is the case, then the mix of personality and behavioural characteristics exhibited by professionals – that have brought us successfully to where we are today – may not be the best combination for the future. If a team-based approach is the way ahead, we suggest that there are ten personal characteristics that are needed. The extent to which these characteristics exist in our current professional staff will give an indication as to how well equipped we are 'people-wise' to succeed in a new way of working.

Equally, we also suggest that effective leadership, motivation, recognition and reward are needed if a firm is to fully embrace a Key Client-focused way of working.

If any or all of these 'essentials' are so foreign or counter-culture to a particular firm, then it has the freedom to choose an alternative future strategy that best suits its natural strengths. The only unacceptable way forward is to proclaim a strategy of client focus but fail to deliver. This makes the professional firm unbelievable. And the one thing a business that sells its expertise must not be, is unbelievable.

FIRST STEPS

If you hold a senior position within the firm:

1. Decide how important client management **really** is to your firm's future success, and therefore what, and who, you are prepared to give up to achieve it.

2. Discover the real values held by people within your firm.

3. Decide what, if any, changes need to be made to align the firm's values to its client management strategy, and then decide if these are possible to achieve.

4. If these changes can be made, then develop those who cannot, or will not 'fit', out of the firm.

5. Ensure that your recruitment and development processes are designed to ensure that everyone embodies the values and behaviours that support effective client management.

6. By implementing the above, reap the rewards in profitable growth.

If you are not in a position of power in your firm:

1. Decide how important client delight is to your own personal success and what you are prepared to do to achieve it.

2. Analyse, honestly, what values the most senior people in your firm hold dear.

3. Decide whether these values are compatible with yours and, if not, decide when you will leave.

4. Make sure that the values and behaviours of the people in any new firm you are considering fit with your own values.

5. By implementing the above, reap the rewards in a successful and fulfilling career.

Appendix:
Key Client Management
Healthcheck Analysis

FINDING THE MOTIVATION

Referring to the statements in the Healthcheck at the front of this book, encircle the relevant score (3, 2, 1, 0) according to which statement (A, B, C, D) most closely matches your firm. Add the individual scores in the right-hand column to gain a grand total, then refer to the analysis below for the verdict on your performance. (As an example, the first grid, below, has been completed as for a fictitious firm.)

Statement no.	Just like us us (A)	Somewhat like us (B)	Not really like us (C)	Not like us at all (D)	Totals
2	(3)	2	1	0	3
6	3	2	(1)	0	1
11	3	(2)	1	0	2
24	3	(2)	1	0	2
30	(3)	2	1	0	3
36	3	(2)	1	0	2
42	3	2	1	(0)	0
				Grand total	**13**

0–7   There is no substance to any initiatives aimed at building relationships with Key Clients. Any initiatives are likely to be driven only by the motive of profit for the firm.

8–15   Whilst your firm may make noises about being client-focused, some of this message is cosmetic. There is still a lot to do at many levels to make the proactive management of Key Client relationships a major focus for your firm.

16–21   The concept of, and belief in, the importance of Key Client management is well embedded in your firm. It is supported from the top and has acceptance throughout the organisation.

CLIENTS, KEY CLIENTS AND CROWN JEWELS

Statement no.	Just like us us (A)	Somewhat like us (B)	Not really like us (C)	Not like us at all (D)	Totals
1	3	2	1	0	
15	3	2	1	0	
39	3	2	1	0	
45	3	2	1	0	
				Grand total	

0–4   Your firm must work out and agree who its Key Clients are, then set about defining exactly what type and level of service will make these clients loyal and likely to buy additional services.

5–9   You have done some work in segmenting your client base, but more needs to be done in relation to defining the most appropriate and fitting type and level of service to delight the most valuable of these clients.

10–12   You are very clear as to who your Key Clients are and you have defined the service you provide them by listening to these clients.

SETTING AND MEETING CLIENT EXPECTATIONS

Statement no.	Just like us us (A)	Somewhat like us (B)	Not really like us (C)	Not like us at all (D)	Totals
19	3	2	1	0	
29	3	2	1	0	
38	3	2	1	0	
44	3	2	1	0	
				Grand total	

0–4   Don't expect clients to pay rewarding fee rates: they have no incentive for doing so.

5–9   The service experience of your clients could be improved with the belief in, and implementation of, some simple disciplines.

10–12   Your firm has (or is building) a reputation for delivering exceptional service compared to most firms in your marketplace.

MARKETING TO CLIENTS

Statement no.	Just like us us (A)	Somewhat like us (B)	Not really like us (C)	Not like us at all (D)	Totals
7	3	2	1	0	
10	3	2	1	0	
16	3	2	1	0	
20	3	2	1	0	
21	3	2	1	0	
37	3	2	1	0	
59	3	2	1	0	
				Grand total	

0–7   You have a lot of work to do if you are going to get any results from the marketing activities you engage in.

8–15   Your marketing activities make a contribution to your firm winning new work, but with more focus and effort your marketing could help you win more work and win it more easily.

16–21   Your marketing is well integrated with your professional activities. It has a positive effect on your clients and you should be able to observe a clear correlation between the marketing events and activities you engage in and the new work your firm wins.

SELLING TO CLIENTS

Statement no.	Just like us us (A)	Somewhat like us (B)	Not really like us (C)	Not like us at all (D)	Totals
9	3	2	1	0	
14	3	2	1	0	
25	3	2	1	0	
28	3	2	1	0	
31	0	1	2	3	
32	3	2	1	0	
43	3	2	1	0	
47	3	2	1	0	
48	3	2	1	0	
60	3	2	1	0	
				Grand total	

0–10   You will often be beaten to new opportunities by firms who really understand what business development through selling is all about.

11–22   Your firm will be competitive in many selling situations, but by really understanding the selling and buying processes more, you could have greater success.

23–30   Your firm is probably one of those that no one wants to go head-to-head with in a straight fight for work.

CROSS-SELLING TO CLIENTS

Statement no.	Just like us us (A)	Somewhat like us (B)	Not really like us (C)	Not like us at all (D)	Totals
13	3	2	1	0	
41	3	2	1	0	
51	3	2	1	0	
				Grand total	

0–3   You probably have little success in cross-selling in your firm.

4–6   You may have some successes in cross-selling but they are not frequent enough.

7–9   Your firm is one of a rare breed. You should be having quite good success in selling in new areas of work for your firm.

FORMING THE PLAN

Statement no.	Just like us us (A)	Somewhat like us (B)	Not really like us (C)	Not like us at all (D)	Totals
18	3	2	1	0	
22	3	2	1	0	
23	3	2	1	0	
33	3	2	1	0	
40	3	2	1	0	
57	3	2	1	0	
				Grand total	

0–6   If your firm is going to take the management of its Key Clients seriously then addressing the Key Client planning process has to be high on your list of priorities.

7–13   You do plan what you want to do with your Key Clients, but there are areas in which your firm's planning could be strengthened.

14–18   There is a lot of thought and effort that goes into planning your approach towards your Key Clients.

USING SUPPORTING TECHNOLOGY

Statement no.	Just like us us (A)	Somewhat like us (B)	Not really like us (C)	Not like us at all (D)	Totals
3	3	2	1	0	
8	3	2	1	0	
27	3	2	1	0	
50	3	2	1	0	
53	3	2	1	0	
55	3	2	1	0	
56	3	2	1	0	
58	3	2	1	0	
				Grand total	

0–8   Either you have no technology or what you have needs to be totally overhauled. The systems in place make little or no contribution to your Key Client management.

9–17   There is still room for much work to ensure your technology totally supports your efforts in managing Key Clients.

18–24   Someone has really put some thought, effort and money into your client management systems.

MANAGING KEY CLIENT RELATIONSHIPS

Statement no.	Just like us us (A)	Somewhat like us (B)	Not really like us (C)	Not like us at all (D)	Totals
4	3	2	1	0	
17	3	2	1	0	
34	3	2	1	0	
35	3	2	1	0	
46	3	2	1	0	
49	3	2	1	0	
52	3	2	1	0	
				Grand total	

0–7   Real teamwork which is needed to manage major complex Key Clients does not happen today in your firm.

8–15   Teamwork in your firm is OK but there are many areas for improvement.

16–21   Your firm has obviously put conscious effort into developing the practicalities of effective teamwork. Your Key Clients probably see a fairly seamless approach from people in your firm.

VALUES AND CHARACTERISTICS IN KEY CLIENT MANAGEMENT

Statement no.	Just like us (A)	Somewhat like us (B)	Not really like us (C)	Not like us at all (D)	Totals
5	3	2	1	0	
12	3	2	1	0	
26	3	2	1	0	
54	3	2	1	0	
				Grand total	

0–4 You haven't really begun to do anything about aligning your firm's values and your professionals' characteristics with a policy of cherishing your Key Clients.

5–9 You are doing something, but there is more to be done.

10–12 Your firm has clearly made a conscious effort to align itself to values and peoples' characteristics consistent with effective Key Client management.

OVERALL EVALUATION OF KEY CLIENT MANAGEMENT AND YOUR FIRM

Total

0–60   If Key Client management is important to your firm in the future, you have a lot to do.

61–130   You have some things in place, but there is much work still to do. Focus on those areas where there is the greatest disparity between where you are today and where your firm would ideally like to be.

131–180 Whilst there may be things you still need to do to stay on top of the process of managing your Key Client relationships well, you should be winning a lot of repeat and new business from your client base. Also, your clients really like doing business with your firm. Seek to improve those areas where you did not score so well.

Index